ALL YOU HAVE TO DO IS BE

On The Path To Fulfilled Personhood

ALL YOU HAVE TO DO IS BE

Tom Caldwell

Library of Congress Control Number:		2006909986
ISBN:	Hardcover	978-1-4257-4310-9
	Softcover	978-1-4257-4309-3

Scripture references marked KJV are from the King James Version of the Bible.

Scripture references marked BCP are from the Psalter of the *Book of Common Prayer*, issued by the General Synod of the Anglican Church of Canada, 1959.

This book was printed in the United States of America.

To order additional copies of this book, contact:
Xlibris Corporation
1-888-795-4274
www.Xlibris.com
Orders@Xlibris.com

37221

CONTENTS

Foreword

"Let each become all he is capable of being."[1]

There's nothing like going right to the heart of the matter. Thus, in some words that "cut right to the chase," the Apostle John addresses himself to every person involved in the essential search for a life that is deep and fulfilling. He writes simply: "What we will be has not yet been made known" (1 John 3:2).

Notice carefully his choice of words. He does not say that "what we might be able to *do,"* or "how much *wealth* or *security* or *celebrity* we might be able to generate," or even "the degree to which we might be able to *impress other people"* are still unknown factors. (Those things, admittedly, all too often represent *our* idea of "what it's all about," *our* view of success or achievement, *our* notion of what gives significance to our existence.) But John takes a different approach, and speaks of something else. He sets forth what he implicitly posits as *God's* idea in the matter, and asserts, simply and pointedly, "It hasn't even been revealed yet what we will *be."* That puts our search for meaningful life into a particular perspective.

Life Can Be Beautiful—Oh Yeah?

I make a sad observation—to the effect that, regrettably, too much attention has been focused on some rather shallow goals of existence in our society—goals such as: the getting of money or possessions; the consistent good fortune to avoid the darker and more painful things in life and to walk for at least most of the time in the sunshine of good fortune; and the attaining and maintaining of a narcissistic sense of inner pleasantness and equilibrium. But if we dig out and examine the principle indicated by St. John, we are gripped by the simple realization that the ultimate experience and apprehension of life's greatest goal does not involve any kind of superficial satisfaction, but, rather, has to do with something much more fundamental and intrinsic to our nature—not *getting,* not *having,* not *achieving,* but the profound reality of *being.*

This involves nothing less than a deep, refreshed and refreshing sense of personal actualization and realization; a profound awareness, centered in the very core of one's person, of coming to be aligned with, and then giving expression to, the very life-principle that God imparted to us, the vital and basic dynamic of our existence. We are called, and invited, and *challenged* to *be.*

That really is the natural goal of our even taking up space on this planet earth, is it not? Indeed, it may be argued that the very term that we use to define ourselves—"human *beings*"—is, in fact, a mandate and a call to a full personhood fully embraced and fully expressed. We are not just human *thing-a-ma-jigs,* or human *whatch-a-ma-callits.* We are God's treasured creations, challenged with the calling, and graced with the title, of human *beings!* "In Him we *live* and *move* and *have our being*" (Acts 17:28); and we feel—(indeed, we may say we "know in our bones")—that we were not designed by our gracious and life-affirming God to live in the dismal swamps of inner emptiness and failure, eking out some pitiful, minimal spiritual and emotional existence, never really knowing what it means to be fully and truly alive. Rather, we believe that we are summoned to move above and beyond the stagnancy and the dead-endedness of inferior, lackluster lives into the vibrancy and worthwhileness of rich freshness and fullness of person. "Leave thy low-vaulted past!" the poet wrote.[2] And we have to shake ourselves loose from what holds us back, to grasp and realize what beckons us on.

How Do We Get To A Life That Is Beautiful?

One of the most gripping and revealing stories in the entire Bible is the account in Genesis, chapter 32, of Jacob's midnight wrestling match with a mysterious stranger. All night long, we read, Jacob and his unnamed opponent grappled and struggled, each vying for mastery over the other. Whether Jacob, in his mighty combat, contended with God, or an Angel sent by God, or, as some have suggested, symbolically with his own inner self awakened by God, it is difficult to say for certain; but one thing is clear. When the morning came and the sun arose, Jacob had resolved the inner conflict that he had needed to come to grips with. He rose, victorious, and went on his way.

It may be that Jacob's experience is something that you and I can know and relate to personally, to at least some degree. Perhaps we, too, have "wrestled all night" with some deep inner concern regarding our life and our aspiring to fullness of being. Or perhaps we stand even now at the point where such a struggle is engaging us and pressing us on in our quest for optimum personhood. Wherever we are in our life journey, my concern is that, like Jacob, we emerge from our striving to grasp more firmly the possibility of realizing our potential for living as full and fulfilled human beings.

Who am I? What is the reason for my being here on earth? What is my vision of my highest and best self? Those are big questions, indeed, and they must not simply be answered selfishly or egocentrically; they must, before all else, be answered honestly and personally. Thus, we start with the assertion, "I am a human *being*, and I am prepared to strive towards realizing and apprehending a life that is good, and fulfilled, and meaningful—in short, a life that is beautiful. But, how do I get there? And—more basically—how do I even get started?"

I'm glad you asked! I want to help you in the pursuit of your destination. I can't give you a map that will unerringly take you there; but I can give you some compass headings that will truthfully steer you towards your goal—and that is really what the rest of this book comprises.

What we will *be*—(what, at the very heart of our persons, we really *want* to *be!)*—has not yet been fully realized and experienced. But, Oh! the joy of finding it out and making it our own! Oh! the joy of entering into a journey of discovery, like a modern-day Columbus reaching out towards, and seeking to apprehend, our own "new world" of personal wholeness and fulfillment!

So—all you have to do is *be!* "But," you ask: "Be what?" "Be who?"—and most of all, "Be how?" Ah! The answer to all that is so complex!—and yet so simple! Let's pursue it together.

Notes

[1] Thomas Carlyle, 1795-1881.

[2] "The Chambered Nautilus," Oliver Wendell Holmes, 1809-94.

Chapter 1
All You Have To Do is Be
ADVENTUROUS

The words with which Jesus commonly addressed those whom He called into a life-search for wholeness and meaning were the ringing words of invitation and demand "Follow Me!" Immediately, thereby, He intimated the nature of the involvement that He was calling persons to. Through that urgent invitation, He showed that what He had in mind was something *active,* not something passive. Finding a life of depth and vibrancy and joy was not going to be an armchair exercise. It was going to be an enterprise of movement and discovery. And that original challenging invitation continues to define anyone's experience with Him. Jesus is always inviting us into the new and the unknown, urging us on into the discovery of new and deepening meaning that lies ahead. He constantly keeps life fresh and open-ended, as He encourages us to move ever forward into the wonder of our own becoming.

Stagnancy Is Not A Viable Option

It was St. Thomas Aquinas who once asserted that there are, in fact, four sorts of existence in our world.[1] There are, Aquinas said, first of all, inert things—like rocks—which simply exist. Then there are those things which exist and grow—like various plants and trees. Thirdly, there are things that exist and grow and move about—like animals. And finally, there are things that exist and grow and move about and *think.* (Guess who!)

Yes, that's us. Created "in God's own image," we are not meant only to exist, or to exist and grow, or even to exist and grow and move about. That would be nothing more than going through the motions of living. We are meant to be in our world in a cogent and participatory way that will lead us to discover and understand and embrace our Creator's wonderful design for us. And if that sounds like a challenge and a call to action, it's because that's just what it is!

Let me comment on this matter of our being actively involved in the process of coming to be fully and blessedly alive in a little different way by sharing with you an anecdote that I first remember hearing many, many years ago. It has to do with the question, "What is the easiest and best way to capture a crocodile?"

You might think that getting one of those fierce, man-eating beasts into captivity would offer a considerable challenge. But, in fact, the method that is proposed according to these instructions is quite easy and simple. All you need is some very basic equipment: a comfortable lawn chair, a dull book, a big shaker full of black pepper, a telescope, a pair of tweezers, and a matchbox. Once you have all of that material together, you're ready to start. And you proceed as follows.

You go down to the edge of a jungle stream where you know there are crocodiles, and set up your chair a stone's throw from the bank. Then you carefully but generously sprinkle the black pepper over the ground between your chair and the stream. That done, you relax in the chair and begin to read your dull book. Pretty soon you are so bored by that book that you fall asleep. Now the plot unfolds. The crocodile, peeping out of his watery hideaway, sees you and notices that you have nodded off to sleep. This gives him his chance to stalk you, so he stealthily creeps out of the water and starts crawling towards you. Naturally, he has to traverse the area that is covered by the pepper that you have spread, and as he does so, snorting and puffing, he inhales a big snout-full of that powerful stuff, which makes him sneeze uproariously. This makes such a terrible noise that you are immediately startled into wide-awake consciousness. You sit up in your chair, let the crocodile get right up to where you are, and then pick up the telescope and look at him through the wrong end. This, of course, instead of magnifying him, shrinks him, so that he looks no bigger than an ordinary grasshopper. With the tiny beast in your sights, then, you take your tweezers, pick up the little crocodile, and deposit him in the matchbox. You then close the lid tightly, and you have captured a man-eating crocodile in a clever and effortless way. (It sure beats the kind of grappling and tussling that Marlon Perkins used to go through on the old *Wild Kingdom* television series!)

Without belaboring the point of the story, suffice it to say that it makes about as much sense to consider actually trying to capture a crocodile that way as it does to imagine trying to find new and thrilling and fulfilling life through the process of being and becoming without setting out on a real adventure of mind, heart, and spirit to follow Jesus.

"A Little Traveling Music, Please"

Let me suggest another insight into this particular way of understanding our calling to be as we seek life's goal. This involves what is probably one of the best known, and yet possibly one of the least understood, sayings of Jesus. I refer to our Lord's own declaration in which He set out the very stark terms under which anyone might make a wholehearted commitment and response to Him: "If anyone would come after me, he must deny himself and take up his cross daily and follow me" (Luke 9:23). Those words lead to a particular form of conjecture.

What did Jesus mean when He challenged His followers to be prepared to pick up their cross daily in their adventure of faith? Was He referring to the terrible practice of that day whereby condemned prisoners on their way to the place of execution were required to carry the very cross on which they would be put to death? Was Jesus thus warning His disciples that they should be prepared to face daily the grim possibility that, because they were followers of Him and His way, they risked death on a cross, just as He did? That, of course, is a possible explanation but perhaps a less likely one than we often assume. After all, at that point in their experience, the disciples would probably not have been able to understand so direct and threatening a reference. They did not anticipate dying on a cross just because they were Jesus' associates. They did not even anticipate that *Jesus* would die that way! Quite the contrary. They were laboring under the assumption that, in fact, Jesus was planning to establish a kingdom of great peace and glory right in the time and place where they were. Reference to the possibility, let alone the imminence, of crucifixion as an outcome of discipleship might very well simply have sailed right over their heads.

Well, then, what do these often-repeated words of Jesus mean? Are they, perhaps, to be seen as a metaphorical, symbolic expression, uttered by our Lord in order to point out the hazards of true discipleship? If so, then we could paraphrase them to mean something like the following. "All those who would follow Me should be prepared to die to the concerns of life that entangle them and weigh them down. Just as a person appointed to death picks up his cross to go forth to that inescapable appointment, so each of My followers must fix his or her eyes on Me and be willing to move unswervingly and single-mindedly towards whatever end discipleship might entail." Such an interpretation would certainly be in keeping with the challenge to whole-hearted devotion that Jesus issues; and many a disciple has found that meaning to be most applicable in his or her own determined resolve to follow Jesus Christ without reserve. Moreover, this also takes into account the requirement to do that sort of thing daily, on a continuing and ongoing basis, and certainly seems to get to the heart of this saying of Jesus. It also leads to a more detailed consideration of the particular wording that our Lord employed.

Consider that, in the original language of the New Testament, the word that is translated "cross" is the Greek word *stauros*. That word is commonly associated in our minds with the Cross as this has been represented in sacred art for us, the Cross on which Jesus died—a two-beamed instrument comprised of an upright stake and a horizontal crossbar. The crossbeam is usually pictured as being nailed to, or perhaps even mortised into, the upright shaft, to form a solid unit. And the terrible apparatus thus configured is, indeed, correctly identified through the word *stauros.*

However, that word *stauros,* as it was commonly used in the first century, did not *necessarily* (and certainly not *restrictively*) mean a two-beamed structure at all. It literally, and more basically, meant simply a pointed stick. In fact, if we were to describe a common twenty-first century picket fence in first-century biblical Greek terms, the word we would use would be *stauros,* because that means a sharp stick, a pointed stake. It can be expanded and added to, to form the "cross" which is familiar to us; but that is not the only way the word was in fact originally understood and applied in common usage.

That being noted, then, consider that, in the terminology of the day in which our Lord set forth this challenge to take up one's *stauros* daily and follow Him, the word *stauros* might also be used, in appropriate context, to mean simply "tent peg"—the "sharp, pointed stick" that would be used to fasten the tent cords of the dwellings of a nomadic people. That adds a whole new dimension to what Jesus was implying about being ready, any day and every day, to follow Him. And it reminds me, actually, of the experience of my own family back when our children were young and we spent our summer holidays tenting, moving from one provincial or state park to the next.

In those days we had a beautiful big family-sized tent that was truly "state of the art"—with an exterior aluminum frame, an adjustable center pole, and some pointed aluminum tent pegs. I well remember our method of operation as we would move into and out of the various campsites we visited. My wife and our daughter, for their part, would be responsible for making sure that all our gear—cooking utensils, bedding, and so forth—was on hand for packing or unpacking; while our son and I would be charged with the work of erecting the tent upon arrival and dismantling it upon departure. We of the tent crew, particularly, had our job down to a science. We could whip that tent up in record time, and/or whip it down just as quickly, as the occasion required. And that included driving the tent pegs in or yanking them out. When it came time to move on from one place to another, there was no hesitation or fumbling on our part. We could have those pegs out and the frame down and our tent packed in as close to nothing flat as it would be possible to get. And that's what comes to my mind when I think of this secondary way of understanding what the word *stauros* might have meant as Jesus used it. "You will need to be ready," Jesus could be understood to be saying, "to pick up at a moment's notice when I give the call. You will need to be prepared any day to pull up your tent pegs, as it were—to take up your *stauros*—and to venture with me into new challenges, new possibilities, new and open ways of looking at and entering into life. Companionship with Me is going to involve new dimensions of spiritual growth and movement, and you need to be ready for that as I call you to it and lead you into it."

That way of viewing and thinking about Jesus' words of challenge concerning cross-bearing says, I believe, something very important about our readiness to respond to the call to *be*. We must always be ready to "pull up stakes," and move with the currents of life as these continually touch us and affect us.

Life Is To Be Exuberantly Experienced—Not Just Tightly Managed

Following Jesus is truly an adventure; and adventure has about it the air of uncertainty and even serendipity. Which means that life very frequently must and will be experienced under the exhilarating rubric, "Ready or not!" Consider the following personal anecdote in this regard.

A number of years ago I was the student minister of two small churches in upstate New York. Both churches had morning worship services each Sunday, and my schedule was designed to accommodate that reality. I used to begin the service at the first church on my charge at 9:45 a.m., finishing in time to drive the five miles over to the second church where the service would begin at 11 a.m. Arriving there, I would enter the church hall to be customarily met by the small choir that sang each Sunday, who would be gowned and waiting for me. After pausing for a brief prayer, we would enter the sanctuary to begin the service. I followed that routine for three years while I served in that setting, for every Sunday that I was on duty—except two. It is those two Sundays I want to tell you about.

One day in the middle of a typically cold, cold upstate winter, I arrived at the second church as usual just before 11 o'clock. I parked my car and walked in through the back door, to be met not, as usual, by the eight or ten members of the choir, but, surprisingly, by the entire congregation, all jammed into the small facilities of the fellowship hall. It seems that the furnace in the church had cut out some time during the night, leaving the temperature in the sanctuary somewhere well below the freezing range and making it impossible to hold the worship service there. This had been discovered by those coming for Sunday School earlier on; and so steps had been taken to make the best of the situation. Instead of holding Sunday School, those present had set about to make the church hall ready for 11 o'clock. The hall was on a separate heating system, and it was warm and comfortable. So, chairs had been gathered from all available classrooms, tables had been moved back, and a makeshift seating area had been set up to accommodate the congregation. And that is why, when I arrived, I was greeted by the unusual sight of a group of people who could have been accommodated comfortably in the larger church sanctuary, all squeezed and sandwiched together in the more cramped quarters of the hall. Everyone seemed to take it all in good spirits, and the close quarters were accepted without complaint. The choir was there, too, faithful as always, and ready to do their part in the worship. However, instead of being easily seated in their customary commodious choir loft, they, like everybody else, were pinched and packed into the accommodation at hand. They had been crammed into one corner of the room in a makeshift arrangement and sat huddled together there, shoulder to shoulder, gamely ready to carry on smiling, nonetheless. So it was, then, that at the appropriate moment in the service they struggled to their feet, stood before that "refugee" congregation, and sang the song that they had rehearsed earlier that week for this particular day. Their anthem, as it turned out, was the glorious affirmation: *"We Shall Not Be Moved!"* The lesson, I assure you, was not lost on any of us who were there in the midst of our makeshift situation! There were a few smiles, and a general sense of appreciation for the wonderful bit of irony that we were a part of. The anthem surely got everybody's attention that day!

That, though, also calls to mind the other unusual Sunday that I also want to tell you about. This one concerns a reassuring message that effectively contrasts with, and yet appropriately goes along with, the uncertainty and open-endedness that the first Sunday so graphically emphasized.

This time the occasion was not a cold winter's day but a hot summer's day. And this time I arrived at the church just before service, expecting to be met inside the church hall by the choir, only again to be surprised; not, though, as before, by how many were there to greet me, but how few. Only one person awaited me: my friend Ron, who was the lone bass in our little choir. He explained the situation to me. Several members of the choir were away on holidays, someone else had a sick child, another person had had unexpected company, and so on, until it ended up that there was not even a quorum of the choir available to perform their anthem. So it had been decided at the last minute that Ron alone would be in the choir loft that day, and that he would sing a solo.

Now, I have been in virtually innumerable church services in my life, it seems; and I have heard virtually innumerable anthems and solos sung in the ministry of music. Many of them have been both moving and memorable. But among them all, I still treasure the meaning and the impact that Ron's impromptu solo had for me that day many years ago. It was no grand aria, no magnificent canticle. Rather, he simply selected a familiar old Gospel Song and sang that as his solo. The words were a tremendous blessing and encouragement to me then, as they have continued to be through all my life since. He sang four verses, all of which are beautiful; but the first verse sums it all up for me:

> My times are in Thy hand:
> My God, I wish them there;
> My life, my friends, my soul,I leave
> Entirely to Thy care. [2]

I can't think of any assertion more filled with assurance and confidence.

"Say the word, Lord," we affirm in our spirits: "Every day, in any way, we're ready to follow You in the spirit of *adventure.*"

Notes

1. See Rollo May, *Freedom and Destiny* (New York: Dell Publishing Company, 1981) p.62.
2. William F. Lloyd, 1791-1853

Chapter 2
All You Have To Do Is Be

BELIEVING

In referring at this point to our need to be believing in our quest for fullness of life, I do not have in mind the outlining of any particular form of doctrine or dogma. I leave that most worthy undertaking to others more didactically inclined. Rather, I am thinking, in this regard, of a single key principle which I wish to present; something so important that without it we will spend our lives wandering around in the swampy lands of ineffectiveness, dissatisfaction and personal failure; something of which it may be said, "Unless you believe *this* and hold steadfastly to *this*, your faith will never lift you and guide you and empower you to the life that you seek." What I refer to is a principle of only three words, representing and embodying what is at once a most demanding and most rewarding basis upon which to build our entire understanding of life. It is the capsule creed: *"God is good."* Consider that brief credo in the light of three statements about the nature and character of life.

Life Can Sometimes Be CONTRARY And FRUSTRATING

When I was growing up in my home town, among my many acquaintances I had one particular friend who had an unusual and personal way of responding to the common greeting, "How are you?" When asked that customary question, he would characteristically respond, with a big smile, "Everything is *peachy-keen!*"

Ah, isn't it nice when that's the way we, too, can greet the world—when we can echo such a happy sentiment and affirm that things are going well, that everything is "coming up roses," and that "the world is our oyster"? Well, in the normal course of events, there will be at least some days for most of us when we can do just that. But, life being in reality what it is, there will also be other days for *all* of us when we *can't*—days when life is anything *but* "peachy-keen." So, what about it when *that* is the case? What about those times when our wires get crossed, and the breaks don't go our way; when I feel short-changed, or badly stung; when my ship doesn't come in, or my number doesn't come up; when I get cut off at the pass, or it rains on my parade? *That* is a different matter. Then I begin to wonder if I am really living in the best of all possible worlds; and then I begin to ask, "Where are the goodness and mercy that are supposed to follow me all the days of my life (Psalm 23:6 KJV)? They must have taken a different road from the one I'm on!"

I am reminded of some words reportedly attributed to St. Teresa of Avila, when she addressed God very honestly in prayer on one occasion of distress and observed, "If this is the way You treat Your friends, no wonder You have so few!" Well, think about it. If we truly desire and seek to be God's "friends" in devotion and obedience, do we or do we not have the right to expect to receive some sort of special consideration from Him in our life struggles? After all, what are friends for? And when no such special consideration is a part of our experience, do we then even dare to ask the Almighty, as boldly as St. Teresa did, "Is this how You encourage people to be Your followers? How come You treat Your friends this way?" Which brings to mind, from a little different angle, a cartoon that I remember seeing once that also says something about what should or should not happen in a Christian's life just because we expect God to do or not to do certain things for us. A young boy is seated at the table with his family; and he has obviously been given the opportunity to say the grace before the meal. He bows his head and prays: "Bless, O Lord, this chicken and this rice which You have provided; and do what You can with this spinach that the devil seems to have slipped in!"

Well, in things much more significant than spinach we may find ourselves frustrated, our plans thwarted, our dreams side-tracked, our efforts foiled and our hopes dashed. And we wonder at such times how come we keep getting slapped down and roughed up and kicked around by life; and we struggle to reconcile our experience with what we know we *should* believe about the goodness of God. And often we end up secretly dubious and maybe even somewhat covertly angry as we think like that. At least, that's what came to my mind on the occasion when my wife and I took a trip several years ago now to the Baseball Hall of Fame and Museum at Cooperstown, New York.

There is tucked away there in the archives at Cooperstown—not on display at the time we were there, because of some further research being done into the matter of its actual authenticity—a certain baseball said by at least some baseball historians to be the very one used in a historic game played away back in the year 1867, involving a player by the name of William Arthur Cummings, known more familiarly as "Candy" Cummings. Candy was one of the pitchers on this supposedly historic day, and he had the usual repertoire of pitches that players of that early time were accustomed to; which meant that he simply stood on the mound, reared back, and let fly with the fastest, hardest throw of which he was capable. An occasional "slow ball" might be mixed in, and the location of the pitches might vary, but otherwise, finesse didn't enter into it at all. The pitcher's job was essentially to overpower the hitter with the high velocity of his delivery or to fool him with an unexpected softer pitch. On that fateful and memorable day, though, Candy Cummings departed from the regular routine of throwing nothing but the two regular pitches. Using a particular grip on the ball, and releasing the ball in a particular way, Candy Cummings is said to have actually thrown the first *curve ball* in baseball history. The effect was remarkable. No one had ever seen anything like it! Something new had indeed been added![1]

Now, I pass on to you that little piece of baseball trivia not just to draw your attention to the fact that there may or may not actually be a baseball in Cooperstown that may or may not be the one actually used by Candy Cummings on a notable day in 1867—although, to a true enthusiast of the history of the game, such an artifact would not be without considerable interest. But, rather, I share this with you in order to also share something else—which is the undoubtedly amazed and chagrined, not to say shocked and angered, reaction of the hitters to whom Candy Cummings served up his newly-created curve ball on that landmark occasion. How unfair and ungentlemanly it must have seemed! One can just imagine the dumfounded batters throwing down their bats in frustrated disgust as they walked back to the dugout, muttering murderously to themselves, after having flailed away at the crazily elusive pitches they had faced!

Little wonder! Always before, those hitters had simply braced themselves for a pitch that would come straight from the mound to the plate. It was part and parcel of the game that the ball would be served up in either the fastest or slowest manner possible. Imagine, then, the astonishment and the distress and the indignation at Candy Cummings' apparent unsportsmanlike behavior in serving up a ball that actually broke its straight trajectory to veer away from, or to turn in on, the unsuspecting batter. Surely such a thing must have seemed outrageously unfair!

Think about that, then, as you imagine the setting being transformed from a contest on a baseball field to the adventure of life, itself. Have you ever heard anyone say—or have you even said, yourself—something that makes the inevitable reaction of those hitters on that day at least a little bit descriptive of our attitude towards some of the things we meet in our search for life's best? Sometimes, just when we really and intensely want or expect some particular thing to unfold or occur—just when, in baseball terms, a hard, straight fast one right over the heart of the plate is what we're primed for—have you ever been frustrated, or let down, or had the ground cut out from under you; and then explained that disturbing and distressing turn of events by employing the metaphor, "Life really *threw me a curve*"? Just like those players facing that unexpected and frustrating pitch thrown by Candy Cummings so long ago, we feel cheated, maligned, and gypped. Only this time it isn't the unfair tactics of an opposing pitcher that we complain about. It's the unfair events of life that we regard with feelings of questioning resentment.

Well, life may be like a lot of things; but one thing it definitely is not like is a friendly game of Slo-Pitch at a family picnic, where everybody gets the opportunity to hit the ball as solidly and as far as he or she can. In fact, we use another expression to acknowledge just that reality. We talk about "playing hardball" in life; by which we mean that this is no longer kid stuff. We're playing for keeps now; and the "curves" of difficulty and opposition and frustration that are sneaked in on us and tend to catch us by surprise and baffle us and botch up our hopes are frequent and unavoidable elements in our struggle. And these things are not to be lamented over or protested against, as though we shouldn't have to face them. Rather, just as a real major leaguer wastes no time in lobbying to have the hard pitches removed from the game, but rises to the occasion and strives to handle the difficult throws that confront him; so we, in life, ought to strive to rise above the "bush league" level of quailing or quitting in the presence of adverse or unpropitious developments. We are meant to face up to those things with courage, determination and persistence; to rise *above* them, yes, to rise *out* of them or *on* them and even *by* them; to take the contrary and frustrating things in our lives and actually turn them to our advantage in our journey of personal growth. But wishing, alas, definitely does not make it so. And, added to life's contrary and frustrating quirks and turns, we have to face an even deeper and harder reality.

Life Can Sometimes Be DISAPPOINTING And DISILLUSIONING

> *"Cheer up," they said: "things could be worse."*
> *So I cheered up, and they were right. Things got worse.*

Sometimes what happens to us is more than just an inconvenience that we can handle, or a letdown that we can come to terms with, or even a knockdown that we can dust ourselves off from to get back up again. Sometimes we experience certain events, or are brought into certain situations and circumstances, which leave us deeply impacted and even terribly hurt through what happens or fails to happen to us. Sometimes we can't just shrug it off. Sometimes we can't just grin and bear it. Instead, sometimes we are led to say with the Psalmist, "I am worn out from groaning. All night long I flood my bed with weeping and drench my couch with tears" (Psalm 6:6). Sometimes our loss and our pain can seem inconsolable. Shakespeare has Hamlet express the depths of despair in eloquent words that bespeak a very common sentiment:

> How weary, stale, flat and unprofitable
> Seem to me all the uses of this world!
> Fie on't! ah, fie! 'Tis an unweeded garden, that grows to seed;
> Things rank and gross in nature possess it merely.[2]

Truly, there will be times when our journey through life will seem to be a cheerless and desolate experience. And it will be at those times that, rather than simply to despair of any help and hope, we will need to turn believingly to the One who assures us always, no matter what, "I will never leave you, or forsake you" (Hebrews 13:5), and assert with the poet:

> Within the maddening maze of things, When tossed by storm and flood,
> To one fixed trust my spirit clings; I know that *God is good.*[3]

But it doesn't end even there.

Life Can Sometimes Be UTTERLY TRAGIC And CRUSHING

There is a place that the human spirit can know that is more, even, than what we sometimes call almost glibly the stereotypical "worst case scenario." There is a place where there just seems to be no tomorrow, when we face life only to find that all meaning seems to have dropped out of it or to have been driven out of it altogether. Sometimes the measure of our loss or hurt or sorrow is so immense that in our affliction we simply lose all hope. All our will or desire to continue vanishes. Emptiness and desolation blanket the heart and spirit. And we are driven to the point of utter extremity where all our bright and positive clichés are replaced by the most heart-wrenching words that human lips can utter, expressed in our Lord's cry from the Cross, "My God, my God, why have You forsaken me?" (Mark 16:4) We look for a glimmer of meaning towards which to direct ourselves; we seek for some sense of God's presence with which to console ourselves; we long for some fragment of ultimate purpose with which to sustain ourselves; but all in vain. We have bottomed out. How can we now affirm, out of our utter extremity, "I believe that God is good"? Can there be any real meaning in those words now?

There may be some persons reading this page who don't know what I'm talking about at this point, who have never touched the borders of utter desolation and forlornness. Perhaps there are some individuals who, in their relationship with God, never lose the light of His presence, never feel the pain of His absence, and never tread the unknown wasteland of forsakenness and dereliction. But for most people, unfortunately, such is not the case; and the biblical record reveals over and over again the normal encounter of the soul, in pursuit of God and goodness, with the tragic and crushing factors of overwhelming emptiness and distress. Read Lamentations, chapter three. "He has driven me away and made me walk in darkness rather than light" (v. 2). "Even when I call out or cry for help, He shuts out my prayer" (v. 8). Sometimes there simply is no light or peace or joy. Sometimes there is only darkness and turmoil and despair. And sometimes it seems as though it all matters very little to God and that it must and always will be so.

The problem of meaninglessness and forsakenness is universal. It can stalk the elderly, in the fading and often lonely and painful twilight of life. It can show itself invidiously as "the destruction that wasteth at noonday" (Psalm 91:6, KJV) to those ostensibly at the height of their powers, blighting and devastating their hopes. And it certainly can cast its grim shadow over even the sunny days of youth and childhood.

A friend of mine told me once of an experience that he had while serving as the minister of a three-point circuit of rural churches. In each of those three churches, which he visited every Sunday, beginning with a worship service at 9 a.m., and finishing with one at 11:30, with the other one squeezed in between at 10:15, there were children present and he told a children's story, using the same story in all three churches. One day his children's talk was built around a question that he asked the youngsters, and their impromptu responses to it. The question was, "What is the biggest thing in the world that you can think of?" This always prompted some eager, innocent, and often amusing replies. And after the children had rather entertainingly participated by setting out such things as, "a mountain," "a big hotel," "the barn on our farm," and so on, my friend would draw the discussion to its intended point by the application of whatever hidden moral there was behind the question—something, in this case, to do with the greatness of God's love and care. Well, things proceeded smoothly as the morning wore on, and in the first two services the children's time was a great success; which brought my friend to the third service, expecting that the story would go over well there, too. And in a sense, it did; but with a different kind of insight being realized. After the question had been asked, and several youngsters had volunteered their answers: "a skyscraper," "a ball park," and so on, my friend the minister observed one little girl who was sort of hanging back in the group and not sharing in the story; so he tried to encourage her to participate as well. "Charlene," he said: "what is the biggest thing in the world that you can think of?"

Charlene responded with a frank and profound answer that was as unexpected as it was grave. Looking at the minister with deep and serious eyes, she spoke with all the tender simplicity that only a little child could express, concerning what was certainly the biggest thing in her world. She said simply: "My mother can't walk!"

"God is good." Do you believe that? *Can* you believe that? It is no sign of failure to be tempted and tested with regard to our faith. It is not wholly exceptional for us to feel at times that the devil has grasped the controls of our destiny and that he is sifting us like wheat in the loss and affliction that we face. I tell you, in such an instance unless we are able to move through even the tragic and crushing aspects of life to affirm, "Yes, Lord, I believe!" we will not be able to find an answer and a resolution to the problem of desolateness and despair. But if we can find the solid rock of confidence in a good and loving God beneath our feet, then we will, as St. Paul exhorts, be ready to "stand firm in the faith" (1 Corinthians 16:13.)

In other words, in its simplest form: All you have to do is be *believing*. Life can and often will seem unfair and harsh and difficult. But that's not the bottom line. The final word is that, in and through it all, *God is good*; and that, by the grace of God and through the grace of God, life can and will be beautiful.

Notes

[1] The Baseball Hall of Fame, Cooperstown, New York, visited 1980. While there is still some debate on the historicity of the curve ball, the official Cooperstown position is reflected in the appropriate plaque there that reads: "W.A. 'Candy' Cummings. Pitched first curve ball in baseball history. Invented curve as amateur ace of Brooklyn Stars in 1867. Ended long career as Hartford pitcher in National League's first year, 1876.'"

[2] John Greenleaf Whittier, 1807-1892, from his poem "The Eternal Goodness."

[3] William Shakespeare, 1564-1616, *Hamlet,* Act I, sc.2.

Chapter 3
All You Have To Do Is Be
CHRIST'S

I want to frame the import of this chapter within a very gracious and prescriptive three-fold claim concerning the Lordship of Jesus—a definitive statement that Jesus made about Himself when He said, simply but sweepingly, "I am the Way, the Truth, and the Life; no one comes to the Father except through Me" (John 14:6). In the light of that declaration, I would go on, then, to say several things about how our Lord relates to us and to our journey towards personal wholeness.

Jesus Christ Affirms The TRUTH About Ourselves And Our Quest For Wholeness.

Consider the following illustration.

Once there was a young lad who lived on a farm, whose ambition was to grow up to be a champion body-builder, exceptionally well conditioned and strong; and in this regard he once had a novel idea about how to accomplish his goal. It started when one of the cows on the farm gave birth to a calf—a frail, spindly-legged little creature barely able to stand on its own. The young man was struck by the difference between the small body of the calf and the ponderous bulk of the cow. One was slight, and easily manageable; the other was massive, and virtually unmovable. Bearing that in mind, he decided that, starting at day one, he would make a practice of going out to the barn and lifting that calf as a daily routine—simply putting his shoulder under it and hoisting it off the ground. That way, as the calf grew, the budding superman's ability to lift an increasing weight would also grow; and eventually, the day would come when he would be able to lift the huge bulk of the full-grown animal. What a thrill it would be to be able to just grab hold, and actually pick up a full-grown cow! But: need I tell you that somewhere along the line that process collapsed into failure? The sad day came when the young man, his biceps bulging out from his effort, and his eyeballs bugging out from his exertion, found himself straining and struggling, heaving and hoisting, grunting and gasping, all in vain. He had reached his limit. He could go no further. His muscles were toned, his thews were thick, his sinews were supple; but his plan was doomed.

That story could be a parable. It could be a picture of our discovery as we address the goal that we have set of becoming and being our best and fullest selves—the sad discovery that even when we have expended our all, even when we have striven with our noblest endeavor, we have nonetheless fallen short, and are unable to attain the completeness of person that we seek. And the reason for that is something that is built tragically into the very greatness and glory which are the hallmarks of our nature.

Very simply, while it is true that we are made in the image of God (Genesis 1:27), and that we are called to show forth the possibilities which are ours through our creation, it is also true that the old story in Genesis where we read about our glorious beginnings does not end on the high and sanguine note of "ever onward and upward." For that old story is, sadly, the story of the failure and the "fall" of humankind. Adam and Eve, the account tells us, ate of the fruit of the one tree in the garden that God had forbidden, thus introducing moral failure; and the profound pervasiveness of that moral failure means that there is more to that story than meets the eye, as St. Paul argues so eloquently in Romans 5 and 1 Corinthians 15. Because of that disobedient action, Paul argues, our first parents—and all who came after them—forfeited the state of original grace and were thenceforth destined to a life marred with circumstantial inferiority and personal imperfection. Call it "original sin," call it an inherited proclivity, call it an innate propensity, it all comes down to the same thing: what went wrong in the Garden of Eden reaches out far beyond its time and place of origin to touch all of humanity and to affect each and every one of us. Accordingly, it is impossible to read the story of Adam and Eve without realizing that we must view it not so much as being a window on ancient history as a mirror on contemporary life wherein Adam and Eve are not the only characters; each one of us is right there, as well, in the middle of the action. *Their* story is *our* story. *Mea culpa.*

As a consequence of our participation in the drama of humankind's "fall" we find our best efforts towards a life of goodness and meaning frustrated. Even though we are human, we cannot seem to reach our goal of being *fully* human. We are mocked and frustrated by our shortcomings and failures. And that brings us back to the particular Scriptural reference which shows the way in which St. Paul dealt with our problem. He talks about how God reveals a plan to help us attain our goal. That plan is, in short, Jesus Christ.[1]

And here we may want to anticipate and even forestall Paul's words through a rather hard-nosed and determined question that the young man in the story above might prompt us to ask, as he may well have wondered where and why his plan went wrong:—namely, "Why can't we just make a go of it on our own in our quest for fulfillment? Granted that in the would-be body builder's case the calf eventually grew to the place where it would have taken a winch or a crane to allow the boy to realize his hopes of lifting it; but, in *our* case—in the much more sophisticated process of *becoming*—if we were to try harder, and concentrate more intently, and practice more diligently, couldn't we finally reach our goal? Do we really need some help beyond ourselves in our efforts? Do we really require the importation of some sort of extra-personal factor to undergird us and equip us in our journey to wholeness? Why can't we just give it all we've got, and go on from here to *become* and *be?*"

So, first of all, Paul deals with that caveat. He sets out the answer—truly a very hopeful and helpful answer from someone who knows personally whereof he speaks. He goes back to the record in Genesis and picks up on the story there. Adam, he acknowledges, came from the hand of God characterized with utter glory and potential—the crown of all of God's creation—Adam and Eve, male and female, representing the perfect wholeness and complementarity of full and radiant human living. *But,* Paul goes on; don't forget what happened to our first parents. They lost their original estate, and the paradigm then shifted so radically that they were henceforth faced with the prospect of living on a level of personal imperfectness, initiating in the process the ongoing problem that has beset every human person who has come after them. And the fact is that, try as we may to deny it or work around it, ever since then humankind just can't get it right because humankind has simply become wrong, and is out of harmony with God and with self at the very center of its corporate and individual being. And remember, Paul was writing out of the background of a very real and bitter personal experience. He was no armchair quarterback in the struggle for wholeness. He knew intimately the profound perplexity of the human condition. "I have the desire to do what is good," he declared in one place; "but I cannot carry it out. . . . What a wretched man I am!" (Romans 7:14,19).

The ancient Genesis story, though couched in non-scientific terms, is a brilliant and incisive exposition of the eternal human condition. What a powerful and insightful way of describing how things are with every human person! You could discourse for hours in sophisticated psychological and anthropological language, and yet never say nearly so graphically and so concisely just what is the reality of our pervasive and prevailing human condition—which some anonymous wit has commented on in terms perhaps less seriously theological, yet also clear and apt:

> Perfection was ours in beginning,
> But we spoiled our chances by sinning.
> We trust that the story will end in God's glory;
> But at present, the other side's winning!

Now enter St. Paul with the words that he has been setting us up for—a particular explication of what the life and ministry and death and resurrection of Jesus all mean for humanity in the light of the Genesis story. "The thing is," Paul writes—and he's simplifying matters, even as I am paraphrasing him—"there's good news, and there's bad news." First, the bad news. Adam, the first human person, did not, as we have noted, maintain the perfection with which God had endowed him. He sinned and failed, and passed on to every one of us a legacy of intrinsic personal wrongness. "Judgment followed sin, and brought condemnation" (Romans 5:16). As a result, we just can't succeed in being what we know we ought to be and what we really want to be. We are, in and by our very nature, sinners. We may slog and stumble along on a journey towards wholeness; we may aspire to a fuller and fuller measure of being—but, to put it bluntly, "we're beat before we start."

Well, that *is* bad news indeed! But Paul doesn't stop there. He goes on in the light of the second thing that our Lord declares about Himself.

Jesus Christ Embodies The WAY To Newness Of Being.

"Now for the good news!" Paul continues. "The good news is that—speaking allegorically—amazingly, there has now appeared a *second Adam!*—someone who has proved to be just as perfect as the first Adam was imperfect, and who, through the representation of Himself on behalf of humanity, has cancelled out for us the blighted heritage that was ours and opened up a new world of possibility in which the old, original promise of *being* and *becoming* is again set before us. And that second Adam is none other than Jesus Christ!"

Something to sing about, right? And we have the words to do so:

O loving wisdom of our God!
When all was sin and shame
A second Adam to the fight
And to the rescue came.[2]

This doesn't mean, now, that because of what Jesus has done we can go back to Eden. No, we have not had the clock turned back for us. Something better! We have had the future opened up for us! It's a philosophical, as well as a theological proposition that St. Paul sets out as he continues to expound the Old Testament story in the light of the New Testament Gospel: to the effect that, just as the First Adam's action was generic, and was the basis for our fall, so the Second Adam's action is universal, and is the basis for our rising to newness of life. "As was the loss, so is the gain," Paul teaches us. "If the many died by the trespass of one man, how much more did the Second Adam's work of giving new life to persons, just like the first Adam's work of bringing death to persons, reach to every one of us?" (Romans 5:17, paraphrased.) Through His self-giving death, wherein He showed that there was no limit to the love and grace of God, and whereby, through His perfect obedience, he reconciled us to God; and through His triumphant resurrection, whereby He opened up the prospect and afforded the power of a personal rising to newness of life, Jesus now extends to every person the glorious possibility of rising above the deadness of our old way of being in the world as we enter a fellowship with Him that is the experience of life that is "life to the full" (John 10:10).

Jesus Christ, it may be said, came to earth on a two-fold mission; namely, to bring *God* to *us* and *us* to *God*. And it was concerning the focus of that ministry that Jesus declared Himself to be not just another way, or an alternate way, but simply *THE* Way. Put in its plainest terms we might simply say that He lived the life that we could not live, died the death that we should have died, and rose victorious over sin and death in order that we might know the life that He has opened up before us. "My Father's will is that everyone who looks to the Son and believes in Him shall have eternal life" (John 6:40.) Think of that! *Eternal life!* That is, the very Life of the Eternal One dwelling in us as it is granted through Jesus Christ! He is the *Way* to the life for which we hunger and thirst.

Now, in that regard bear this in mind. Such a statement is not an arrogant and peremptory rejection and dismissal of all non-Christian efforts to know God and live a worthy life before Him. Rather, it is, really, a reverent effort to assert the incredible profundity and comprehensiveness, and the declared veracity and validity, of the claims made about Jesus. "He is before all things, and in

Him all things hold together" (Colossians 1:16). The Christian understands and believes the wonderful truth that—not in a narrowly *ex*clusive way, but in a gloriously *in*clusive way—"God was in Christ reconciling *the world* unto Himself" (2 Corinthians 5:19 KJV, emphasis added). "The Lord is patient . . . not wanting anyone to perish, but *all* to come to repentance" (2Peter 3:9 KJV, emphasis added.) No one, on any honest biblical grounds, could presume to limit or curtail the activity of God in relating Himself to persons in ways unknown, and perhaps unknowable, to us. "God was pleased through Him to reconcile to Himself *all things*" (Colossians 1:20, emphasis added); "He made known to us the mystery of His will according to His good pleasure to bring *all things in heaven and on earth* together under one head, even Christ" (Ephesians 1:10, emphasis added). The details of such divine activity are within the province of God's prerogative, not ours; but there is a broad and essential perspective here that needs to be asserted and understood. We need to see and acknowledge something very basic about Jesus Christ the Lord; namely, that that is precisely who He is—Jesus Christ the *Lord!* Oh, He is an Example and an Exemplar and an Inspiration, as many would be prepared to acknowledge—but He also goes far beyond any and all of that. He is not just someone who happens to be able to give us a leg up on our human situation by giving us a fresh start; and He is not, either, simply someone who demonstrated for us how to live as we ought, setting a pattern that we must now endeavor to emulate. He is far more than just a heavenly Role Model, exemplifying ultimate human personhood. Rather, far more gloriously than that, He is the One who came to *redeem* our fallen human personhood in order to restore us to our destiny in God; and it is His risen and redeeming presence and power that we receive as He comes to us to deliver us from our broken and imperfect past and liberate us to a new and fulfilling future. And in the effecting of this, it is to be not just Christ for us, or Christ with us, but—as St. Paul puts it in Colossians 1:27—"Christ *in* you, the hope of glory."

That is why the Gospel of God's redeeming action in Christ is so vital to any approach to whole and meaningful living. Otherwise, we could still find ourselves struggling under the impossible burden of trying, like the young man I mentioned in beginning, to raise ourselves to a level of personal accomplishment that is, in fact, beyond our strength to attain. And that is why we need to lift our eyes even beyond the level of mere "personal fulfillment," as desirable as that may be, to the heights of the glorious salvation that God offers to each of us—the knowledge of sins forgiven and the promise of divine companionship in our daily living. And, finally, that is why the preaching of John and Charles Wesley and their followers, for example, was predicated on one insistent, urgent and compassionate plea: "Let me commend my Savior to you!" He is the *Way* that sets us free.

To Know Jesus Christ Is To Know LIFE Indeed

The life that Jesus gives has been characterized in various ways and has been experienced in different ways, as well. The one thing that is common to every experience of Christ's redemptive action for any person is the realization that something new and transforming has occurred. The Bible expresses this through the use of various figures of speech. For instance, when Christ's gift of new life in the soul is granted to any seeking individual, it is equated with, say:

- *(a)* Coming out of darkness into marvelous light (Ephesians 5:8); or
- *(b)* Awaking from a sleep to a new and vibrant consciousness (Ephesians. 5:14); or
- *(c)* Being freed from the dungeon of a prison into glorious and exultant liberty (Luke 5:18); or
- *(d)* Being ransomed and restored after having been held captive (Matthew 20:28); or
- *(e)* Having all charges against you dropped as you stand condemned in a court of law (Colossians. 2:13-14); or
- *(f)* Being born all over again (John 3:5-7); or
- *(g)* Coming home to a loving, forgiving welcome after having foolishly and perversely wandered away (Luke 15:21-24); or
- *(h)* Being healed of blindness and/or deafness, to be able to see and/or hear life's beauty for the first time (Matthew 11:5);
- *(i)* And *so on.*

Almost every conceivable human image that could somehow shed any light on the idea of a free redemption bestowed by a gracious Lord is pressed into service in the Scriptures in the hope of striking some chord to which some person—*any* person—might be able to respond by saying hopefully, "That's what I need to have happen to me;" or by affirming appreciatively, "That's what I experienced when the Life of Christ came to me."

And that great event occurs, when it is actually apprehended in any life, sometimes vividly and dramatically and instantaneously; and sometimes incrementally and gradually and almost imperceptibly. But as the drawing and claiming and winning influence of the Spirit of God is expressed towards us, the wonderful thing is that it *does* happen; and we awake, ultimately, to the realization that because we have opened our hearts to Him, Jesus Christ has kept His promise and has come in to us to live and to dwell with us, thereby imparting to us His life (Revelation 3:20). That life is now within our very soul; and the simple confession that arises from that knowledge and that experience is: "I am *His* and He is *mine*."

Notes

[1] See Romans 5:6-9, which I am using at length in an interpretive rendering.

[2] J.H. Newman, 1801-1890, "*The Dream of Gerontius,*" 1865.

Chapter 4
All You Have To Do Is Be
DISCIPLINED

Whenever most of us hear the word "discipline," the tendency usually is for us to associate it with a struggle to control, contain, or keep within determined limits some activity, practice or habit. Such things as diets and New Year's Resolutions come swiftly to mind. But I want to think beyond that to something that is related in a much more profound way to who and what we are as living, meaning-seeking selves. We live under worthy discipline as we seek to be true to our most profound inner reality, and as we strive to govern and direct ourselves unswervingly to the progressive discovery and affirmation of that reality. In that light, consider the following.

There Is The Discipline That Concerns SELF

Jesus once asserted a principle having to do with who or what might receive anyone's ultimate loyalty and be the guiding and driving force in anyone's life: "No servant can serve two masters" (Luke 16:13). It's that simple. You can't give your undivided attention to one insistent purpose while still looking out of the corner of your eye at something else and trying to give part of your concentration to that as well. You can't play both ends against the middle and expect to do justice to either end, or to do anything else but mess up the middle. You can't go in two directions at once, no matter how fancy your footwork. Try it, and you end up being a "double-minded" individual, (James 1:8), dragged and tugged back and forth by the fitful tides of divided loyalty.

I recall a story about a man who apparently had gotten himself caught in just this sort of thing when he borrowed twenty dollars from his friend, Joe, promising to pay it back in one week. The week went by, and the borrower found that he had no money with which to repay his loan. So he went to another friend, Jim, and borrowed twenty dollars from him in order to reimburse Joe, promising Jim that the loan would be paid back in one week. That week went by, and our borrower unfortunately now found that he had no funds with which to repay Jim. So he went back to Joe who, on the strength of the earlier transaction, again lent him the money, due in one week. This then allowed the borrower to repay Jim, but left him in an ongoing quandary. He couldn't seem to get out of the vicious cycle within which he now found himself. Each week he ended up borrowing twenty dollars from either Joe or Jim, as the case might be, in order to repay the twenty dollars received previously from Jim or Joe, and so on. This went on for weeks and weeks, with the man seeming to get nowhere. Then one day, as he was walking along the street, he saw both Jim and Joe coming towards him; and he was struck with an idea. Bringing the two men face to face with each other, he introduced them to each other, and then pleaded, "Why don't you two guys just get together each week and leave me out of this whole thing?"

But life isn't that simple—though it can seem, at times, to be that complicated! We can never get on with the job of discovering and attaining our own fullest personhood as long as we constantly are dividing our attention and our commitment between our highest goal and something else that we keep encouraging and sustaining. We have to pay off either Jim or Joe, as it were, and concentrate on either Joe or Jim, or we'll always be in debt to a shallow and unsatisfying way of life. And I say that advisedly, fully aware that this is no merely hypothetical concept that we face. "Life is real, and life is earnest;" and conflicting options and impulses often seek very strongly to draw us to very different loyalties.

> To every man there openeth
> A Way, and Ways, and a Way;
> And the High Soul climbs the High Way,
> And the Low Soul gropes the Low,
> And in between, on the misty flats,
> The rest drift to and fro.[1]

Sometimes the worst that we may feel is that we have deliberately and even shamefully chosen the Low Way; or the best that we may feel is that we're still somehow no more than drifting to and fro on those misty flats of in-betweenness; while the pure goal of the High Way stands unpursued and unattained. And the clamoring *self* that prefers inferior ways continues to impede us and weigh us down. It is a self that is willing to settle for mediocrity or shoddiness or even impurity, and that strives to foist those things upon us as satisfactory life goals.

Myself, arch-traitor to myself,
My hollowest friend, my deadliest foe,
My clog whatever road I go;
God, harden me against myself,
This coward with pathetic voice
Who craves for ease and rest and joys.[2]

Domination by self can be depressing, especially when I have determinedly made all kinds of resolutions, and all kinds of promises to myself to turn over a new leaf—and failed. I've given in, or caved in. I've backslidden. Let's face it; I can no more pay off my own haunting, oppressing Joe or Jim than I can pay off the staggering total of the national debt! And yet there is no reason to despair, because there is some tremendously Good News for me to hear! My inferior, obstructing self can be disciplined and overcome! I can rise above the misty flats of aimlessness and turn away from the Low Way of meanness to ascend the High Way of being and becoming! That is the Gospel truth. That's the Gospel *promise!*

Yet One there is can curb myself,
Can roll the strangling load from me,
Break off the yoke and set me free.[3]

"Thanks be to God!" St. Paul exclaims. "He gives us the victory through our Lord Jesus Christ"(1 Corinthians 15:57).

It is not our own self-generated strength of intellect or will power that enables us to discipline our demeaning or disruptive or destructive selves. "I can do all things through Christ which strengtheneth me" (Philippians 4:13 KJV), St. Paul wrote, enunciating a vital and pivotal truth. Our discipline is not a discipline of accomplishment, attained by grim determination. It is a discipline of relinquishment, attained by allowing the Spirit and the power of Jesus to pervade our lives and give us insight, direction and enablement for living.

There Is The Discipline Related To CIRCUMSTANCES

One of the commonest rejoinders given to any challenge to overcome the negative forces of life and to press on towards *being* and *becoming* is the disclaimer that, while it may be possible for others to undertake such a glorious quest, it is not possible for me because of my particular circumstances. It looks good on paper, as they say, but I can't venture forth on the quest for fullness of being because things in my life just don't allow it. I am boxed in, or bogged down, or blocked off in a unique way by insurmountable obstacles that simply shut me down before I can even get started. *"I can't, because."* That's the first part of the formula employed by the person who immediately exempts or excuses himself or herself. And that makes it both possible and safe to add the second part then, which says, *"I would, if only."* Which of course is not really true; because as long as circumstances are accepted as the reason for being a non-becomer, there will always be an endless supply of them to fill the bill as reason enough for opting out. Solve or settle one set of circumstances; and another one just as bad, or worse, will be wheeled in to take its place. No; circumstances are not to be adjusted or corrected or smoothed out into some optimum situation. Circumstances are to be *overcome* and *conquered* as we follow the discipline of living out the life we are promised in the Gospel.

I'm not saying that circumstances are unimportant or that they ought not to be of concern to us. What I am saying is that circumstances ought not to be a deterrent to us in whatever we are called to do and be as a part of our journey to wholeness. And that applies to any circumstance which we may care to consider—all kinds of issues, and concerns that might prompt us to refuse to become who we are called to be until these things are resolved. We could make a list that could start with the most general societal factors and concerns and run all the way down to the place where it all has to really start to get into gear, right down to the singular circumstances and conditions of my life. "I can't really get underway in a full response to the call of Jesus; I can't live in disciplined fellowship with Him—*because.*" Maybe it's the people around me who impede me. They don't understand, or they don't care. They're not supportive. In fact, maybe they're even opposed to my setting out on my venture of *becoming*. Or maybe it's my job. Or maybe it's my health. Or maybe it's my lack of education or social opportunity. Or maybe it's my age. Or maybe it's some combination of some or all of such factors, or even something totally different from any of them. I don't know all the combinations and permutations of circumstances that are possible. And, understand, I'm not trying to make light of what may be for any person real and significant difficulties. I know that there are some persons who will read these words who may face factors of actual and profound hardship, limitations, disadvantage, opposition and maybe even danger. But something else needs to be added to even that comment; which is this: that an expression we sometimes use to justify our lack of attainment—the phrase "under the circumstances"—puts the matter incorrectly. We should be talking instead about how we are going to get *"over* the circumstances"! "I can't because" is often only a fancy facade, constructed of fear or hesitancy. Its counterpart, born in a spirit of determination and hope, should be, "I will, *in spite of!*" And, "I would, if only" can also be simply a smoke screen with no substance behind it. Its counterpart of resolve and discipline would be, "I will, *nevertheless!*"

Many years ago, as a small boy, I saw an example of the way in which circumstances might be addressed that impressed me deeply and has continued to be an influence on my life. It had to do with a one-legged man riding a bicycle. And if that sounds ludicrous, I hasten to assure you that it is anything but.

When I was about eight or nine years old I attended two Sunday Schools each week. In the morning I was present at my own Sunday School in my own church; and then, in the afternoon, I attended a mission school operated in a rented hall by the Salvation Army. Some of my friends were members there, and I used to attend with them. I remember, among the volunteer staff who conducted the meetings, one man in particular who was present faithfully each week, taking part in leading and teaching. The only name I ever heard him called was "Brother Gene." He was a man probably in his early fifties at that time—a layman, though, like the loyal soldier he was, he wore the Salvation Army uniform. He lived about eight miles away in the city of Windsor, and it was necessary for him to travel that distance each week in order to serve and help out at the mission. In those days hardly anyone owned or drove a car, it seemed, unless they were extremely well off, which Brother Gene was not. So he rode a bicycle; which would not have been particularly noteworthy if it were not for the fact that he had only one leg! His left leg had been amputated well above the knee, and he made his way around on a pair of crutches. Now, I think it would simply have been common sense for Brother Gene to assume that, no matter how much he might have wished to help out in the mission Sunday School, circumstances just made that impossible. How could a one-legged man, with no car and no one to give him a ride, travel eight miles each way every week without fail to take part in that activity? The most hopeful response he might have been able to make to that question would surely legitimately have been: "I would *if only*, but I can't, *because!*" But the truth is that he did rise to the challenge, *nevertheless* and *in spite of!* And the way he did it was a marvel to see.

He had an arrangement on his bicycle that consisted of a strong piece of an old automobile inner tube connected from the crossbar to the right pedal—the pedal he could manipulate—so that when that pedal was pumped, it was automatically drawn back up into position for pumping again without any action being required from the left pedal. This allowed Brother Gene to propel himself with considerable efficiency, and, as it proved, with grace and agility. It was wonderful indeed to see this man mount and dismount from his bike. He would store and unstore his crutches along the diagonal bar of the frame, swing himself on or off the saddle, and be ready either to ride away or get off, all the while balancing perfectly on his good leg as needed—all so naturally and effortlessly that it hardly occurred to any observer that this should be regarded as anything but the kind of thing that went on all the time. And though Brother Gene finally rode away into the distance out of my physical sight for what proved to be the last time, he has often reappeared since in my mind's eye. Sometimes when I am tempted to falter in the face of the most untoward circumstances, I call to my mind the determination and the discipline of Brother Gene. Everything about his situation fairly shouted, "You *can't,* because!" But he *did,* nevertheless! And he reminds me anew of the truth that it is possible to be something positive and to become something worthy even in the face of seemingly overwhelming odds. It isn't Brother Gene's actual accomplishment that I remember today, though that is noteworthy. It's the *discipline* that allowed him to go ahead and do what he could—or *couldn't!*—that is an inspiration to me. He showed that it is possible to conquer circumstances.

There Is The Discipline Related To ATTITUDES

Perhaps the greatest factor in Brother Gene's accomplishment was one that preceded his actual addressing of his physical circumstances—which was his disciplined conquering of his *attitude.* And maybe this is what it all comes down to anyway; maybe all discipline really comes down to the determined conviction that the life of *being* and *becoming* is so worthwhile, and the call of God to fully redeemed personhood is so valid, that one must do as Jesus instructed when He spoke of answering the call to life, and simply put one's hand to the plough and allow no doubt or danger or disillusionment to deter one (Luke 9:62). This truly is critical; because the essential factor impeding us so often is, indeed, nothing other than our *attitude.* We don't see ourselves as becomers. We feel unworthy, or unable, or unfit, or unprepared. God's promise is seen as being for somebody else, not for us, and we resign ourselves to virtual imprisonment within a defeatist attitude, bound and fettered by what William Blake described as "mind-forged manacles."[4] And we sit around vaguely wishing that we could be different and that our level of personal being could be higher; but doing nothing about it because we don't really believe that we can. What we want is nerve and verve, and spontaneity and creativity, and *élan vital* and *joie de vivre.* But what we end up with is stagnancy and dullness, and deadness and mediocrity, and *laissez faire* and *deja vu.* And that's all we'll ever have, until we are able to come to a place of determination and discipline and really believe that, by the grace of God, we can move ahead in the venture and the journey of *being* and *becoming*; until, in short, we come to conquer our *attitude,* and live with effective determination.

There is no magic formula, no secret "abracadabra" that will do all this for us instantly and painlessly. But there *is* a simple prescription that will lead to the glorious outcome for which we long. It is the prescription set forth by a wise man of old: "Let your eyes look straight ahead, fix your gaze directly before you. . . . Do not swerve to the right or the left." (Proverbs 4:25,26). In other words, discipline yourself to hold this thought and this attitude: that I am on the journey to *becoming*; that that's where I should be because that's where God told me I belong; and nothing—but *nothing!*—is going to deflect me or dissuade me or discourage me in the pursuit of my goal.

God has already made abundantly clear *His* choice in the matter for us. "I know the plans I have for you," declares the Lord; "plans to prosper you, and not to harm you, plans to give you hope and a future." (Jeremiah 29:11).

Let it be said about us as God's action towards the righteous is described in the Book of Job: "He openeth . . . their ear to *discipline*" (Job 36:10 KJV, emphasis added.) A response of iron-willed determination on our part to seek God and His promise will enable us to live overcomingly as we walk in His way.

Notes

1. John Oxenham, 1852-1941, "The Ways."
2. Christina Rosetti, 1830-1874, "Who Shall Deliver Me?"
3. *ibid.*
4. William Blake, 1757-1827, "London," in *Songs of Experience,* 1794.

Chapter 5
All You Have To Do Is Be
ENTHUSIASTIC

I share with you two incidents from two different congregations in their observances of a particular season of the Church Year. One has to do with the service on Palm Sunday in my home church, for which I was present; and the other comes out of a service a week later, on Easter Sunday, originating as a telecast from a large church in a major city some miles from where I live, which I watched after the fact via videotape.

There was one striking difference between those two worship services that impressed me forcibly. It had nothing to do with the relative sizes of the sanctuaries, or the numbers of people present, or what the choirs sang or what the sermons said. It simply had to do with the matter of *enthusiasm.*

The first service, on Palm Sunday, included a brief presentation by the young children of our Church School. Armed with full fronded palm branches, they were there to sing a song based on the Triumphal Entry of Jesus into Jerusalem, accompanying their song with shouts of "Hosanna!" in an act of praise and adoration, and waving their palm branches almost as flags, as we traditionally suppose might have happened on that day so long ago. This they did; and then, as their part in the service ended, they moved out along the aisles to the accompaniment of music, still shouting "Hosanna!" and still exultantly waving their palm sheaves as they made their way out of the sanctuary and downstairs to their junior congregation, their jubilant shouts trailing noisily behind them all the way.

To say the least, those boys and girls played their parts with gusto, really pulling out all the stops! Talk about *enthusiasm!*—a dozen little sprites entering totally into the experience of worship, giving it everything that they had!

That, as I said, was on Palm Sunday. And then, seven days later, on Easter Sunday, after I had shared in the glory of worship on Resurrection Day in my own church, I sat later in my living room at home and watched a videotape of the Easter worship of a great congregation in one of the leading churches in this part of the country. There were three ministers leading the service that day in that large congregation; and one of them did something that set up the note of difference that I observed between the two venues of worship of which I speak. One minister—one of the two Associates—announced as the opening hymn that morning Charles Wesley's glorious Easter paean, "Christ the Lord is ris'n today," and invited the congregation to rise and to sing heartily that great Christian affirmation. And then, to provide a tangible opportunity for the people to express their joy, he also announced a departure from the traditional way in which that congregation regularly worshipped. A small bell, he noted, had been provided for each worshipper along with the order of service. Those bells were meant to be rung as a signal of rejoicing during the singing of the opening hymn, specifically, in the refrain at every place where the word "Alleluia!" appeared. The idea was that the voices of that great congregation would be complemented by the hearty ringing of nearly a thousand bells; and the result would be an enthusiastic expression of a joyful noise unto the Lord. "And," the minister added in a spirit of good humor and with a touch of levity that I think was intended to free up the congregation for the procedure he had outlined, "just so that I won't be the only ding-a-ling here on the platform, I have a bell for each of the other two ministers as well." Whereupon he outfitted the other two men with little bells of their own—much, I observed, to their surprise, not to say their consternation! Then the congregation rose to sing their triumphant song of rejoicing and to punctuate that song with their "Alleluias" and the literal ringing out of the good news. At least, that was the theory behind it all. In actual fact, it turned out rather differently.

Maybe it was just too unusual an exercise for the worshippers there that day. Maybe years and years of reverent and decorous worship had so ingrained themselves in those present that it was not easy, and maybe not even possible, for them to act with an unaccustomed display of freedom and exuberance. At any rate, when the appropriate moments came, hardly any person there even faintly tinkled, let alone heartily rang, his or her bell. And even the other two ministers seemed too inhibited to participate in anything other than a token way. One of them just held his bell in the hand that supported his hymnbook, and sort of dipped the book a little on the "Alleluias" in a rather gratuitous but stiffly ineffective motion; and the other kept his bell straight down at his side and sort of flicked a finger at it at the appropriate places, almost as though he were trying to shoo a fly away from the side of his robe.

Well, the "Alleluias" got sung, to the glory and praise of God, which was certainly the main thing; but throughout that great sanctuary the bells that were supposed to highlight and emphasize the exclamations of praise barely got rung at all. And that's where the sense of difference arose for me, between this service that I was watching on my television screen and the one in which I had participated just the week before. Oh! I thought; if only the boys and girls from our little church could have been present in this church and gotten their hands on those bells! Then you'd have heard such a ringing, and such a shouting of "Alleluias" as to shake the very rafters in a display of real enthusiasm that would have rocked you right back on your heels!

"Whatever you do," St. Paul advises, "work at it with all your heart!" (Colossians 3:23). "Keep your spiritual fervor!" (Romans 12:11). You'll be so much more successful and effective in your efforts; and you'll have ever so much more fun!

Enthusiasm Is Not Excessiveness, Emotionalism, Or Mere Ebullience

Let me, however, add a necessary note of qualification to what I have just said, to this emphatic effect: that something is not necessarily better or more valid or more worthy of approval than something else just because it is done or presented in a more agitated or energetic manner. That statement is true about many things in general and certainly about worship in particular. God is not necessarily more appropriately honored, and human spirits are not necessarily edified to any greater degree, through worship that bears the stamp of excitement and flamboyance than through worship that is solemn and reserved. The waving of palm branches and/or the ringing of bells, for example, in and of themselves, may be indicative of a vital and profound level of worship being expressed; or, conversely, they may have nothing at all to do with the true quality of what is going on. It is the attitude of heart and spirit that underlies such practices that is of critical, defining importance. We must always remember that, apart from the unseen realities that accompany all inter-relationships between the human and the divine, no true worship is offered or takes place. We need, for the full expression of worship, to realize and rejoice in the mighty presence and power of the living God in the midst of His people touching their hearts with flame and rousing their spirits to a joyful and expressive awareness of His person as God is worshipped, according to our Lord's direction, "in Spirit and in truth" (John 4:24). And to that end, what we do or do not do, and how we do or do not do it, must serve the purpose of allowing the experience of worship to be as genuine and profound as it may be. But be advised in this regard on two counts.

One is that the experience of God's revealed and vibrant presence is not something to be manufactured by us in a worship service or anywhere else. We can't coax, compel or coerce God into being at our disposal as we wish. Rather, our desire ought to be that *we* should be fully at *His* disposal, and then He can come to us as He wills.

And the other caution I would stress here is that we ought, indeed, to receive and worship our Lord pre-eminently and primarily in any and all settings and circumstances, usual or unusual. To put it in modern parlance, we need to "keep our eye on the ball," and see beyond the incidentals of any event or occasion in order to enter both enthusiastically and appreciatively into any opportunity to encounter the One who is the source and vitality of our life. And in this regard, I think of something that happened in the life of a certain young minister very early in his career—something from which any preacher or worshipper might learn a very important lesson.

This young man was in his first pastorate and was still learning to come to terms with some of the demands of leading worship and then standing up to preach before a group of people whose eyes and concentration were solely on him. Such singular attention made him nervous; and he regularly found himself feeling tense as he stood in the pulpit, as many persons who have spoken in front of an audience can understand and appreciate. Some would say that he was suffering from "stage fright." So, he sought some means to try to lessen his stress and to dissipate some of the tension that he felt. And the means that he hit upon was very simple. It was something based on an elementary understanding of physical and psychical energy. He knew that, when you are nervous before an audience as you stand behind a podium or a pulpit, it helps to grasp the stand in front of you and to hold on to it firmly and strongly. Many speakers, especially beginning or unseasoned ones, do just that, almost instinctively. They grab the lectern and hang on for dear life! This not only provides the nervous speaker with some measure of support so that he or she won't collapse like a pile of wet spaghetti on the floor; it also actually serves beneficially to drain off some of the nervous tension which is transferred physically to the object being grasped. Well, so far so good; except that the young man in question happened to be a very strong, muscular individual who had formerly entered and won some prominent competitions in bodybuilding. He was staunch and sturdy and physically powerful.

Well, the fledgling preacher stood before his congregation that day nervously excited and tensed up, energized almost to the place where, like

Galahad of old, "his strength was as the strength of ten." Ready to declare God's Word, he began to speak his sermon, standing solidly behind the pulpit, grasping that pulpit on either side with his huge, strong hands. Ah, that pulpit! It was a lovely hand-made piece of sacred furniture, joined in a V at the front, in a manner faintly reminiscent of the prow of a ship. Someone had lovingly created it and presented it to the little church back in the founding days of the congregation, and for years there it had stood. But after that day, it stood no more.

That day, as the preacher braced himself for his speaking, his hands fastened on either side of the pulpit, his arm and shoulder muscles exerting their force in an effort to abate his nervousness, suddenly there was a crunching, splintering sound—the rending, ripping sound of wood being torn to slivers; and the preacher found himself literally ripping the pulpit in half and standing there suddenly before his congregation with the shattered evidence of his strength clutched in his big fists, looking for all the world like what Samson might have looked like after he had just ripped out the gate and gate posts to the Philistine city! (Judges 16:3). All at once, the preacher was no longer an objective figure safely ensconced behind the comfortable barrier of the pulpit. Instead, like some wild, apocalyptic avenger, he was toweringly and ominously *upon* his surprised congregation, the shattered and jagged remnants of the pulpit that had previously separated them dangling brokenly from his brawny hands! And if at that precise moment he had shouted dramatically, *"Hear ye the Word of the Lord!"* it might almost have been more than his startled parishioners could have borne! This was no drowsy, humdrum sermon that no one would really hear or long remember. This was a sermon where the preacher not only "got through" to his listeners, but where he literally *"came* through" to where they were! There was something powerful and electric in the very air as the preacher eagerly emerged from his shell to share his Good News with the people!

Well, it certainly is not necessary to smash up the furniture for God to be honored, and for God to make Himself known to the waiting heart! But an appropriate measure of *enthusiasm* is necessary.

Enthusiasm Is The Compelling And Impelling Force That Drives Us And Leads Us On Into Thrilling Living

It is not too extreme a statement to assert that the vital factor which makes the difference between *"blah!"* and *"wow!"* in so much of what we do in life is nothing other than *enthusiasm;* and by way of illustration of that assertion, there's a lesson to be learned from the biblical recounting of an interaction between Elisha the prophet of Israel and Joash the king of the nation, as the death of Elisha drew near (2 Kings 13:14-19, summarized and paraphrased).

Elisha, who had been the spiritual stay and advisor of the kingdom, knew that he was dying; so he called Joash to him in order to reflect with him on the future of the country, particularly in the face of a looming crisis with the nation of Syria. There was going to be a confrontation between the forces of the two states, and Elisha wanted to prepare the king psychologically and emotionally for victory.

"Take a handful of arrows," Elisha directed; "and as you think of the enemy, and the battle that will take place, strike the arrows on the ground."

Joash did as he was instructed. He took the arrows in his hand and sort of tapped, softly and hesitantly, three times on the ground—no more than a token compliance with what he had been told to do. And, the Bible says, Elisha was immediately very upset and even angry at the king for what he had done.

"You should have smitten five or six times!" he said. "You should have struck the ground forcefully and vehemently as a symbol of the vigor of your attack on the enemy! That way, you would indeed have handled them with decisiveness and dispatch, and won a great victory. But now—because you have shown such little verve and enthusiasm, because you just did the whole exercise so diffidently and perfunctorily—the outcome is going to lack the quality of clear and complete triumph it would otherwise have had." Someone once said very appropriately, "Life is like a troop of cavalry. It has to be used dashingly, or it might just as well be sent out to pasture to graze!" For dashingly read *enthusiastically*, and you've got the heart of the matter.

Enthusiasm Gives God A Chance To Act In Enrichment And Blessing In Our Lives

"Ask, and it will be given to you; seek, and you will find; knock, and the door will be opened to you" (Matthew 7:7). So said Jesus, encouraging His followers to use boldness and confidence in their seeking of life's best. Don't stand timidly behind the door; don't sit mutely by without even piping up; and don't give up your search and your pursuit. Rather, address the asking and seeking and knocking processes in life with enthusiasm; go for the goal ardently and earnestly and with profound anticipation; because that, and only that, truly opens the way for God to bless you with a life-enriching satisfaction of your quest.

I recall a simple and common incident from our family life that pictures for me the notion of enthusiasm and the difference in any person's approach to life that enthusiasm generates. This happened when our children were quite small, on a pleasant summer day when they had been playing outside in the morning and then were called in to lunch. Now, it happened that both children had been very active in whatever games they had been playing, and that those games had involved some rather hectic running and jumping. Hence, they were still rather keyed up, even after they had come in, gotten washed up, and were sitting at the table. Our daughter was especially still in an excited and dynamic mood. In fact, as she sat on her chair it was almost as though one could still hear her motor humming away.

We all sat down at the table, and prepared to give thanks for our food, as usual. It happened that this time it was our daughter's turn to say the grace; and as the three others of us sat there in reverent anticipation, she did the honors by simply acting out of the state of heightened excitement that had characterized her outdoor activity. Without hesitation she bowed her head and sort of barked out the single word, *"GO!"*

Now, I am not someone to criticize the practice of extempore prayer! But I did feel that perhaps a grace before a meal should be somewhat more structured and pointed, and so I appreciated the fact that, without breaking stride, as it were, the diminutive pray-er immediately went on to say—from her heart, I was sure—"I mean—thank You Jesus, for this food; Bless us now and make us good, Amen." But I must say that the thing that impressed me most about that incident, the thing that has stayed with me over the years and causes me still to recall that occasion so vividly, was the spirit of *enthusiasm* that impelled a little girl to burst out so honestly and so vigorously in her expression of thanks for life and its gifts. And I sometimes wonder if my own prayers and my own attitude towards and participation in life in general might sometimes better serve both myself and others if I could allow more of the *élan vital* that is in me by the grace of God to make its way into who I am and what I do! And in this respect, perhaps I need to hear echoing in my ears some words of our Lord, when He held up a worthy example and said tersely and forcefully: "Go and do likewise!" (Luke 10:37.)

Chapter 6
All You Have To Do Is Be
FORGIVING

Forgiveness is not an option in our lives in the world. It is absolutely vital to any experience of personal and community wholeness, and must be, as it were, breathed in and breathed out like the very air around us that sustains us. We, ourselves, need to be forgiven; and we, ourselves, need, then, to be forgiving. Consider how and why this is the case.

Forgiveness Is The DEMONSTRATION Of Grace

Forgiveness originates with God; and in His case it is entirely gratuitous, in the best and highest sense of that word. God forgives us not because we have somehow earned it, not because we have made up for our sins by canceling them out with a sufficient number of good deeds, not, even, because we are sincerely sorry for what we have done and promise that we will try not to do it again. Rather, God forgives us because forgiving, above everything else, is what He *wants* to do! He is One who "delights in showing clemency"(Micah 7:18). It is an exercise in which He finds the deepest and purest pleasure. We don't have to beg God for forgiveness; we don't have to wheedle or whine before Him or try to bribe Him or impress Him. We just need to receive from Him the forgiveness that He so readily waits to give us. Forgiveness is the unmerited, unconditioned extending to us by God of His pardoning, receiving, affirming love. That's what Jesus taught; and that's what got Him into so much trouble.

Consider the story of The Prodigal Son, as Jesus related that in Luke's Gospel (Luke 15:11-32, with paraphrasing). The prodigal was guilty of that which needed to be forgiven. His conduct had been flagrant and grievous; he had willingly and stubbornly acted in a way that was wrong. He knew that, and he knew that his actions needed to be dealt with and set right. So he determined to do something about it; and he worked out a plan. "I will get up and go to my father," he thought;

"and I will say to him, 'Father, I have sinned against heaven and against you; I am no more worthy to be called your son'"—a statement of real and rare beauty in its honesty and humility. Off he went, then, with the determined purpose in his mind to get himself forgiven and restored. "Now, when I get there," he mused to himself: "I'll lead right off with that speech that I've rehearsed a hundred times: 'Father, I have sinned against heaven and against you, *et cetera, et cetera.*' Then," he thought, "since I've forfeited any right to sonship through my highhanded self-will, I of course won't ask to be accepted and restored and given my place again within the bosom of the family. I can't expect *that!* No, I'll just ask if they're hiring right now and if there's maybe an opening somewhere where I can catch on, some low-level or even entry-level place where I can plug in, so that I can at least hang around and feel that I'm not totally rejected. I'll say, 'Father, just treat me as one of your hired hands.'"

Well, you know the story. Even before he got home, while he was still just a dot on the horizon, the father, who had been waiting and hoping for his lost son to return, spotted him in the distance and ran out joyfully to meet him. The boy began his rehearsed speech, but only managed to get a part of it out. Before he could finish, he was cut off by his rejoicing father who was laughing and crying at the same time, who embraced him and received him and loved him. "Never mind all that!" the father was saying. "Just stand still and let me look at you! Welcome home! Welcome home!" And then, in a sweeping pronouncement of full restoration, he turned to the nearby servants and ordered that his son be clothed in clean and splendid garments, that a ring of celebration be placed on his finger, and that a feast of rejoicing be held to mark this great and glad occasion. "My son is back!" the father declared. "I thought I'd lost him, but now I've found him. That's all that matters. Let the party begin!"

And that's a picture of the way *God* stands ready to receive and forgive *us,* Jesus declared. "I am concerned for you, and will look on you with favor" (Ezek. 36:9). There is no need to fear what kind of reception we'll get: He's waiting and watching for us to return to Him. We don't need to try to mitigate His anger at us or moderate His displeasure with us over what we have been and what we have done. As far as He's concerned, our return means that all of that is in the past. Nor do we need to assume that we'll be given some mean or minimal measure of restoration, as though we have lost any title to a full and loving relationship with Him. So, once we were lost! The main thing now in God's mind is that we are found; and there is rejoicing in heaven that reaches out to touch and to thrill our souls.

That's the way it is, Jesus said. That's how God operates. So why wouldn't simply everyone want to receive the gift of forgiveness so graciously extended?

The answer to that is what led Jesus ultimately to a Cross. "Too easy!" some people said. Others declared, "It doesn't make the sinner pay for his sins!" Still others joined in, "It isn't even fair! It gives the sinner just as much fellowship with God as a righteous person who has conscientiously tried to toe the line and walk the straight and narrow path all of his or her life. Where's the justice in that? Why shouldn't a returning sinner have to settle for a second-rate place? He or she ought to consider himself or herself lucky to be received by God at all!" "Take your story back to the drawing board, Jesus," yet others summed the matter up. "We don't want to hear about some scheme for personal wholeness where a sinner can just waltz right in and be reconciled to God. We want a salvation that demands something of the penitent, not a simple forgiveness that grants grace to anyone who asks for it!"

Jesus, of course, did not go back to the drawing board with His teaching about God's forgiveness. He kept on making the most outrageous kind of declarations about full, free, amazing grace. And as for those who thought that the sinner should need to put a lot more into his end of the bargain, providing some tangible evidence of worthiness, Jesus summed up His view of human efforts at obtaining salvation through works: "This is the work of God: that you believe in Him whom He has sent" (John 6:29). And as far as doubting whether or not anyone would be welcome, even persons who might really have no valid expectation that their application for grace would be favorably received, Jesus simply stated: "Anyone who comes to Me I will never turn away" (John 6:37). And as far as any penny-pinching attitude on God's part, doling out His forgiveness grudgingly or stingily, Jesus simply asserted: "If you then, who are evil, know how to give good gifts to your children, how much more will your Father in heaven give good things to those who ask Him!" (Matthew 7:11). It just couldn't be any plainer.

Forgiveness Is The BESTOWING Of Grace

Forgiven persons are uniquely qualified and profoundly motivated to pass on to others the grace that they have received; to bestow upon others what has been demonstrated to and for them. To that end forgiven persons are also *forgiving* persons. That's what St. Paul indicated in some very straightforward words when he wrote, "Be kind and compassionate to one another, tender-hearted, forgiving each other, just as in Christ God forgave you" (Ephesians 4:32). How can I, who, myself, have received such accepting and affirming forbearance and forgiveness from God, deny the same sort of grace to others who need it or seek it from me? In all good conscience, I really can't. In fact, logically, it is just in view of the profound forgiveness of wrongs and offences accorded to me that I find it both possible and appropriate to pass that Christlike action on.

All of which is usually easier to say than to do. Forgiveness may be a joy and a delight to God. It may be the deepest intent of His person and the richest expression of His will. But for ordinary, frail and broken human beings, it all too often just does not seem to be something the doing of which comes very naturally, or the offering of which brings very much pleasure. Human beings very frequently do not find it easy to forgive. It can be something that they may just feel unable to do; or else it can be something that they just plain don't want to do. At any rate, many of us often seem to work hard at proving that it's something that is basically not natural for us to do!

I once saw a cartoon in a magazine years ago, picturing two young boys who had obviously been playing rather boisterously in the house. It's the sort of situation where you know very well that their parents have cautioned them often enough before, "Be careful, and go easy, or you'll break something. You have been warned!" Well, unfortunately, though perhaps not unexpectedly, that warning has not been heeded carefully enough, because the two boys are standing in the midst of a rather tossed-about room, staring guiltily and somewhat fearfully down at an expensive-looking lamp that is lying broken on the floor. The older of the two speaks, and utters a desperate observation. "The way I see it," he says, "we ask for either a broom; or a ten minute head start!" Sound familiar? Most of us have been on both sides of that predicament at one time or another; and we know both the righteous anger of the avenging offended one and the guilty fear of the one who has been caught red-handed. And I'm not trying to obscure the course of justice here. I'm not denying that there are times when a certain price has to be paid for certain inappropriate actions. But I am trying to put into perspective just how and why a quality of straightforward and outright forgiveness might more often and more fittingly be brought into the human equation. Because, remember, it is a *human* equation. And the thing we need constantly to remember is that the situation of people in relationship with people involves something that is of far more significance to God, as well as to us in our saner moments, than any offended feelings or upset protocol or stepped-on toes or general attitude of being miffed. Maybe you feel you really have someone "dead to rights." But don't forget, that's exactly where God had you! Remember? We were literally "as guilty as sin" before Him. And that's when He granted forgiveness to us. Period! No hanging on to His future rights to charge us or hold us in condemnation; no grudging retaining of the rap sheet, just in case He might want to slap us with it again. Case closed! Can we do the same thing towards others? Can we really pray, "Forgive us our sins to the same degree and in the same way that we forgive those who have sinned against us"? (Matthew 6:12, paraphrased).

Charles Haddon Spurgeon, the great English preacher, tells the following story.

> I recollect . . . an incident that occurred in my own garden. There was a dog which was in the habit of coming through the fence and scratching in my flowerbeds, to the manifest spoiling of the gardener's toil and temper. Walking in the garden one Saturday afternoon, and preparing my sermon for the following day, I saw the four-footed creature—rather a scurvy specimen, by the way—and, having a walking stick in my hand I threw it at him with all my might, at the same time giving him some good advice about going home! Now, what should my canine friend do but turn round, pick up the stick in his mouth, and bring it, and lay it down at my feet, wagging his tail all the while in expectation of my thanks and kind words! Of course, you do not suppose that I kicked him, or threw the stick at him any more. I felt quite ashamed of myself, and told him that he was welcome to stay as long as he liked, and to come as often as he pleased. There was an instance of the power of non-resistance, submission, patience and trust in overcoming even righteous anger.[1]

Nobody likes to have sticks thrown at him or her, figuratively or literally. But I have a recommendation to make that could well revolutionize human relationships if we were ever able to carry it out. Which is, simply, that in instances where we have the occasion to respond to certain actions that we might normally perceive in less than a welcome or favorable light; when someone has launched some perhaps unprovoked or unjustified attack at us when we were innocently just doing our job or minding our own business; shock everybody around you just as the dog shocked the preacher! "Pick up the stick," so to speak; and, to mix in another metaphor, deliberately turn it into an olive branch. Give the gracious gift of *forgiveness!* It will save a lot of grief in the long run; it will give you a spiritual and emotional lift in the process; and it will increase the possibility of the kingdom of heaven actually coming on earth.

Forgiveness Is At The HEART Of Grace.

"To know all is to forgive all." "There, but for the grace of God, go I." Such statements point up for us the graciousness, and necessity of forgiveness. There will never be a time when we do not need to offer grace to others by deliberately forgiving them instead of carefully pressing our claims against them. Even the tenderest relationships—and maybe even especially the tenderest relationships—need this grace. I remember seeing a greeting card meant to be sent by a wife or husband or sweetheart to the object of his or her dearest affection. It carried, on the front, the touching sentiment, "I love you more today than I did yesterday." Then, inside, there was this further comment: "Yesterday, you kind of got on my nerves!" Thank God for people who are willing to bear with me, and endure me, and forgive me, and, yes, *love* me, even when I sometimes get on their nerves! And thank God, He gives me the opportunity to do the same for others, when it's my turn to find something wrong about somebody else's words or deeds. When, too often, our natural inclination may be to respond in kind when we are offended; when the unworthy thought "I'll get even" crosses our mind; when someone "owes" us an apology; when the danger of ongoing ill-will threatens to disrupt any relationship; then is the time to make a clean sweep of the situation by employing the healing grace of forgiveness. Truly, we need to learn to spread forgiveness around. There's not much danger that too much of it will get loose in the land!

Notes

[1] Charles H. Spurgeon, *Spurgeon's Lectures to His Students,* edited by David Otis Fuller (Grand Rapids: Zondervan Publishing House, 1945) p. 395.

Chapter 7
All You Have To Do Is Be
GOOD

"Howe'er it be, it seems to me, 'Tis only noble to be good." [1]

I wonder. I wonder what the result would be if you were to take a random poll of persons in our society, asking the question, "If you could be anything in the world that you wanted to be—what would you choose?" I wonder how many people might respond to that by answering: "I would like to be *good.*" Maybe that *is* the noblest thing that we could wish for. But I suspect that, nonetheless, it wouldn't even be in the top ten of desires expressed by people at large. "I would like to be *rich.*" That one I could predict as showing up in many instances. "I would like to be *famous.*" That, too, I think, would get quite a run. "I would like to be *popular.*" Why not? But—"I would like to be *good*"? How often do we think about *that,* and long for *that?* Seldom, I think. And yet, the quality of goodness permeates the very value systems by which we live and underlies any hope for a truly worthy expression of what it means to be fully human. We need the qualities of genuineness, and moral trustworthiness, and honor, and virtue that true goodness represents and generates within the mix of our daily living. And we need persons to embody and express those qualities in themselves and in their deeds—*good* persons—or else our world will literally fall apart at the seams. That's what Jesus said: "You are the salt of the earth; and you are the light of the world" (Matthew 5:13-14). Without the preserving influence of salt, putrefaction and decay would set in. And without the illuminating quality of light, everything would be darkness all around. Being rich or famous or popular would be nice! But what we need as a foundation for all other desired goals or ambitions is the basic energy and influence of *goodness.*

So let's look at the statement that we're using as a guiding dictum in this part of our consideration—"I want to be *good*"—and let's analyze it a little more thoroughly by looking at several things that it is sometimes taken to mean.

"I Want To Be SELF-RIGHTEOUS And PIOUS"

This is the goody-goody approach to life that many persons see as comprising goodness. (Of course, very few people would actually express themselves in precisely those words; but that is basically what their approach to life declares.) In this view, I am "good" only as I manage to distance myself from what I perceive as the grubby not-so-niceties of everyday life. It is an affected way of being in the world, often adopted in order to impress other people with my rectitude and my righteousness, and often carried out with reference to some ideal self that I would like to represent as being who I really am. What matters more than anything else, often, within this posture is not necessarily how truly interiorly worthy I am, but how outwardly impressive and exceptionally virtuous I can appear to others to be. There is a most revealing statement made in Shakespeare's play, *Othello,* concerning the impression that a worthy person can make on those around him or her. Iago, the villain, closely observing Othello, envies him the quality of his character; and comments, "He hath a daily beauty in his life that makes me ugly."[2]

Perhaps we have all known people of whom we might have said the same thing—people who were, in fact, genuinely and meaningfully *good;* whose goodness unwittingly served as a mirror within whose depths we saw reflected back not our own goodness but our own comparative ugliness. Well, some persons aspire to be considered as just that kind of individual, striving with might and main to create a virtuous impression; which inescapably and indubitably involves two things. One: the certainty that they will fail in making such a worthy impression—at least in any more than a fleeting or superficial way—because, in fact, the goodness that inspires recognition and conviction in other persons who observe and evaluate that goodness is a humble, inwardly-generated, and truly unconscious quality arising not from any deliberate effort to draw attention to itself but from something fundamental within the depths of the soul and spirit of the good person. And two: not only will a genuine impression of goodness not be generated, but, in fact, quite the opposite may be the case. The person acting with a sanctimonious demeanor will frequently be viewed—one could almost say will frequently be *spotted*—as someone superficial, indeed, as—to use the ultimate condemnation that society employs in such cases—a hypocrite. And the studiously affected "good" person may end up turning other people off and leaving other people cold and even driving other people away through his or her unfortunate phoniness. Consider an old but appropriate story: Once, it is said, a young boy was going from door to door in his neighborhood in a search for old bottles that he might turn in to raise money for his boy scout troop.

He came to the door of one house where his knock was answered by a stern and righteous-looking matron. "Got any old beer bottles, lady?" the boy asked hopefully. The lady drew herself up to her fullest and most imposing height and asked with self-conscious, not to say self-righteous, severity, "Do I look like the kind of person who would have any beer bottles in my home?" "Oh, sorry, ma'am," the boy replied, hastily changing his approach: "Got any old *vinegar* bottles?"

"I Want To Be SPIRITUALLY-MINDED And DEVOUT"

This would certainly seem to represent an improved approach to our subject. To say that what I would really like to be in my involvement with daily life is "spiritually-minded and devout" sounds as though I am setting out a high and worthy ambition. My goal in this regard would then be to fix my mind on heavenly things and to live on earth as a citizen of heaven; to rise above the fleeting concerns of earth, with all its mundane minutiae, to live in an atmosphere of prayer and to walk in a sense of loving fellowship with God. And there is a certain degree of validity and empowerment to such an aspiration—as well as a very real sense of falseness and ensnarement.

The New Testament does exhort Christians to live by a set of values and standards that reflect the kingdom of God, and not just the expediencies of our own time: "Set your minds on things above, not on earthly things" (Colossians 3:2). And St. Paul further advocates being governed by a power that transcends the dictates and even the requirements of the present: "Do not conform any longer to the pattern of this world" (Romans 12:2). And devout souls of all ages have sought to heed such injunctions by allowing the things of the spirit to dominate both their thinking and their acting. This is commendable; so much so that it is not really a question of *if* such an attitude should be brought to bear in the affairs of everyday life, but, rather, *how* such an attitude ought rightly to be embraced and lived by in the world. But, a word of caution and advice here; beginning with a comment on what must surely be paradoxical and even oxymoronic in its very essence: the matter of being heavy-handed in spiritual matters.

Charles Spurgeon tells of an experience and an impression of his concerning a certain group of persons committed to a particularly spiritual way of life:

> The Christian . . . should also be very cheerful. I do not believe in going around like certain monks whom I saw, who salute each other in sepulchral tones, "Brother, we must die;" to which lively

> salutation each lively brother of the order replies, "Yes, brother, we must die." . . . Upon the whole, that might be about the best thing that they could do! But, 'till that event occurs, they might learn to use some more comfortable form of salutation.[3]

I think that if Mr. Spurgeon were writing today, he might use a more colloquial term, and simply admonish those earnest brothers to "lighten up!" Which is good advice. Remember that you are, after all, a *human* being; and as a participant in human affairs, it's all right to enter into human involvements and human concerns and simply embrace the situation you are in for itself without trying to shade it over into something more spiritually acceptable by lugging in some dutiful reference to more heavenly things. We do well to remember, as St. Paul once asserted, that God "richly provides us with everything for our enjoyment" (1 Timothy 6:17). Jesus knew that, and gladly accepted and acted it out; so much so that there were those who criticized Him for His apparent "worldliness" and His readiness to enter so fully into the everyday affairs of human living. There were some who would have felt more comfortable had Jesus abstained from some occasions of human involvement, to do something more "spiritual" instead. Well, life can be lived from a spiritual bias, and in fact is truly lived at its fullest and best when that is the case; but nobody has to "come on like gangbusters" on every occasion and in every instance just to assert a bent for goodness based on being heavenly-minded and devout.

Then there is the matter of deliberate separateness from that which is less than admirable or worthy. If I am a devout and spiritually-minded person, surely I have a responsibility to distance myself from wrong actions, impure words and unworthy associations. After all, the Bible warns us to abstain from even the very appearance of evil (1 Thessalonians 5:22 KJV). And we are expressly exhorted by both the Old and New Testaments in this regard: "If sinners entice you, do not give in to them" (Proverbs 1:10); and, "Religion that God our Father accepts as pure and faultless is this . . . to keep oneself from being polluted by the world" (James 1:27). If those admonitions mean anything at all, they certainly mean that the life of a person seeking to be good will have points and occasions of contrast and even contradiction and oppositeness to the life of a person whose mind and spirit and conduct are characterized and governed by inferior motives and goals. Sometimes it seems, as Paul says in Philippians 2:15, that we are in the midst of "a crooked and depraved generation." What, then, is a person seeking wholeness and fullness of being through worthy and good living to do? St. Paul goes on in the same verse to provide an answer. You are to be involved with the people and events of society; you are to act and interact with and within the currents of life around you; but in a particular way. You are to "shine like stars in the universe" in the midst of the very setting wherein you assert and express yourself. "My prayer is not that You take them out of the world, but that You to protect them from the evil one," was Jesus' petition to His Father concerning those who would seek to follow Him (John 17:15). So that's where we are—in the midst of the often exciting and inviting, and sometimes dirty and dangerous, business of common, everyday living. Because that's where God has placed us; and that's where we may aspire to be *good* persons. Truly, and simply, "Jesus bids us shine."

"I Want To Be LIKE JESUS"

Now, that's quite a thought! In fact, it's the highest kind of goal to which we might aspire; and it is precisely what we are urged to seek for in the very plain words of the New Testament: "Christ left you an example: it is for you to follow in His steps."(1 Peter 2:21)

Following "in the steps" of Jesus! That verse from 1 Peter is one that has found reverential expression in hymnody, prose and poetry over the centuries since it was first written; and nowhere more powerfully or influentially than in the ministry and effect of one book in particular, written in the nineteenth century. In 1896, Charles M. Sheldon wrote the inspirational novel, *In His Steps,* subtitled, *"What Would Jesus Do?"*[4] (This was many years before the modern day movement which has adopted that subtitle—or at least its initials—as its slogan was thought of.)

The book told the story of a group of people who agreed to live for a stated period of time with the example of Jesus as their inspiration and model. Specifically, they were to subject all of their living, in all details of business, pleasure and society, to the scrutiny of one overriding provision: "What would Jesus do if He were me in my position? What would He say? How would He act? What would I expect from the One who was the only perfect person ever to grace our earth?" The idea of such a commitment was not to make carbon-copy pseudo-Jesuses out of those who were so involved; not to round off every problem to the lowest common denominator of some pre-conceived Christian formula. That would only have been to put the experiment on a legalistic footing, restricting, or stultifying, or infringing upon the individuality of the participants, and denying them both the freedom and the responsibility of working out their own salvation. To the contrary, rather than being a set stock of procedures to be followed by rote, it was to be simply a governing principle that was to be at the heart of all of their thoughts, words and deeds. In this light, then, Charles Sheldon sets up an exchange between one volunteer for the program and the instructing pastor, as the experiment is about to begin. The volunteer is looking for some clarification of the rubric, "What would Jesus do?"—and the pastor tries to give her some help. The conversation goes as follows.

> (The parishioner says:)
> "I am a little in doubt as to the source of our knowledge concerning what Jesus would do. Who is to decide for me just what He would do in my case? There are many perplexing questions in our civilization that are not mentioned in the teachings of Jesus. How am I going to tell what He would do?"
>
> (The Pastor replies:)
> "You remember what Christ said, speaking to His disciples about the Holy Spirit: 'Howbeit, when He, the Spirit of truth, is come, He shall guide you into all the truth.' . . . There is no other test that I know of. We shall all have to decide what Jesus would do after going to that source of knowledge."[5]

That book became a world-wide best seller, whose influence was felt, and continued to be felt, well into the middle part of the twentieth century until, with the waning of the optimism of the liberalism out of which it seemed to have been born, *In His Steps* has now passed into the category of a relic, reflecting a mindset and a hope of a time that is past. But its essential message is still one of both beauty and power, and, in fact, may still be the simplest and best answer to the persistent and recurring problems of evil and suffering faced by our world. And its hopeful prospect surely still has the power to thrill the mind and soul of both the aspiring individual person and a broken and needy world. Here's how the book concludes, after a long, and complex, and difficult working out of its challenging motif:

> He—(the pastor)—thought he saw the Church of Jesus . . . open its heart to the moving of the Spirit. He thought he saw the motto, "What would Jesus do?" inscribed over every church door, and written on every church member's heart. . . . He saw the figure of the Son of God beckoning to him and to all the other actors in his life history. The figure of Jesus grew more and more splendid. He stood at the end of a long flight of steps. "Yes! Yes! O my Master, has not the time

> come for this dawn of the millennium of Christian history? Oh, break upon the Christendom of this age with the light and the truth! Help us to follow thee all the way!"
>
> He rose at last with the awe of one who has looked at heavenly things. He felt the human forces and the human sins of the world as never before. And with a hope that walks hand in hand with faith and love, . . . laid him down to sleep, and dreamed of the regeneration of Christendom; and saw in his dream a church of Jesus without spot or wrinkle or any such thing, following Him all the way, walking obediently In His Steps.[6]

Well, perhaps it is the idealism of Sheldon's book that has sent it to the sidelines in the life and thinking of our society today. But that does not obscure the fact that Jesus still represents the highest and best pattern and example to which we might ever aspire. We cannot *be* Him, or even be *the same* as Him; for He is the singular person of the Son of God. But we can aspire to be *like* Him in our own discovery and apprehension of what it means to be a son or daughter of God within the human dimension. We can listen to His teachings, we can allow His principles and precepts to instruct us and direct us. We can live out of our own integrity, from the true center of our own personhood, speaking the truth and doing the truth with strength and purpose and dignity, as Jesus did; refusing, as He refused, to be bullied or lured aside in our following of the light. In short, we can aspire to an awareness of, and a surrender to, the person of the living God that will soak through to, and seep into, every fiber of our persons, making us reverent, responsive and ready to do His will.

Jesus' life stands before us as the divinely expressed revelation of a fully-potentialized humanity. To be His follower is surely to aspire to bear the stamp of His nature and His character—to be, in short, *good.*

Notes

1. Alfred Lord Tennyson, 1809-1892, "Lady Clara Vere de Vere" in *The Lady of Shalott and Other Poems* (1833).
2. William Shakespeare 1564-1616, *Macbeth,* Act 5, scene 1.
3. Charles H. Spurgeon, *Spurgeon's Lectures to His Students,* David Otis Fuller, editor (Grand Rapids: Zondervan Publishing House, 1945) page 152.
4. Charles M. Sheldon, *In His Steps* (New York: Grosset and Dunlap, 1935).
5. *ibid.,* p.18.
6. *ibid.,* pp. 244-245.

Chapter 8
All You Have To Do Is Be
HELPFUL

No life can ever be truly meaningful and adequately fulfilled that does not have about it the quality of service and contribution of some sort. Our very nature as beings in community leads us to want to look to the welfare of others who are on the journey of life with us and to act in some way to be a help and a blessing to them.

Helping Is UNIVERSAL And OBLIGATORY

The very fact of our inter-relatedness and interdependence, the very fact that we are all, without exception, "people who need people," means that we all need to help and be helped by each other. From the very earliest moment in sentient human history, from as long ago as that ancient occasion away back when Cain first asked the rhetorical question, "Am I my brother's keeper?" (Genesis 4:9), we have all instinctively known the answer to that query to be "Yes;" and the unfolding story of our race has been, in a very simple sense, the saga of how well we have learned, or how tragically we have failed to learn, that lesson.

Martin Buber relates a beautiful Hasidic tale:

> *When It Is Good To Deny The Existence Of God*
>
> Rabbi Moshe Leib said: "There is no quality and there is no power of man that was created to no purpose. And even base and corrupt qualities can be uplifted to serve God . . . . But, to what end can the denial of God have been created? This too can be uplifted through deeds of charity. For if someone comes to you and asks your help, you shall not turn him off with pious words, saying, 'Have faith and take your troubles to God!' You shall act as if there were no God, as if there were only one person in all the world who could help this man—only yourself."[1]

The "pious words" used in the foregoing story—"have faith and take your troubles to God"—are dismissed as unworthy in this instance because they suggest no more than a readiness to avoid any responsibility on the part of the speaker. But those words are not always entirely amiss, since there certainly *are* heavenly resources we ought not to hesitate on occasion to recommend: just as there certainly are other *human* resources besides ourselves that we should also be ready to draw on. It's always nice to be able to refer! But even so, there are very few cases where we cannot—even in some small way—make a difference through our own words and actions. And in many instances that, and just that—our own words and actions—are what we are called on to give and ought to be ready to give.

> They might not need me; but they might.
> I'll let my head be just in sight;
> A smile as small as mine might be
> Precisely their necessity.[2]

Helping Centers On PERSONS, Not Just THINGS

One of the saddest features of our all too superficial modern living is the fact that we all too frequently turn helping into an impersonal activity that can be accomplished at arm's length through the provision of appropriate resources or instrumentalities. If there is some cause or even some family or person to which or to whom we truly desire to be of help, more often than not our method of helping is to give some thing towards whatever the cause may be. And usually the thing we give is money. "Take this amount of dollars," we say, or "take this check or money order; and with it accomplish what needs to be done to help other persons. It is not even necessary for me to know any of the details. This is my contribution to charity. Now let it work!"

Far be it from me to try to dissuade persons from giving money to agencies or institutions that are engaged in turning that money into words of encouragement and deeds of compassion. I'm not even hinting that there might be too much of that going on! No, my argument is with the idea that impersonal check-writing or money-giving by itself can fulfill the challenge and privilege of being helpful. Jesus' story of the Good Samaritan is a case in point. What our Lord commended in this parable was not the fact that the Samaritan supported a worthy cause by giving a nice donation to the fund for poor, waylaid travelers, but the fact that one concerned person took the time to be aware of the plight of someone else and to actually reach out and be of tangible and present help and support to that other one.

After the verb "to love," it has been said, the verb, "to help," is the most beautiful word in the English language. And the reason for that is that, in fact, it is the verb "to help" that actually proves and establishes the claim of the verb, "to love"—that properly conjugates it, if you will. The best way for me to show that I love you is for me to simply care enough about you to be willing to help you. All of which sounds very noble; but we need to bear something in mind about how this sort of thing actually gets worked out in your ordinary life and mine.

Oh, sure, we can imagine striking situations where we might very dramatically be able to rise to the opportunity to be caring, helping persons. The only trouble is that those obvious and well-focused situations only seem to arise in books or on television programs, where the story line is clear-cut and the protagonists know exactly what they're doing. (And it always helps if there's some particularly moving or melodramatic music playing in the background, too!) But—I can't remember when was the last time that was actually the case with me. In fact, I can't even remember when was the *first* time that was *ever* the case with me! That's how it is with average, garden-variety people like you and like me. Nothing out of the ordinary ever seems to happen to us—no drum rolls, no trumpet fanfares, setting the scene for some stellar action of response on our part. That's why, not a keen eye to pick out the moments when we should act significantly, but a caring attitude that leads us to live helpfully constantly, is what we need to bring to the ordinary littleness of our lives. For it is out of the caring help offered within the often seemingly trifling and unimportant moments that lasting and gracious significance comes. Let me illustrate what I mean by sharing with you a personal experience that had a profound and lasting influence on me

When I was in high school many years ago, one of the courses that I took in grade nine was the one known simply as "Shop." It actually was comprised of four separate segments, each taught for one quarter of the school year by a qualified teacher-tradesman in a particular field. Those fields were: electricity, auto mechanics, woodworking, and machine shop. It was while I was involved in the last-mentioned subject area that an incident occurred that I have never forgotten.

Machine Shop was taught by a middle-aged man affectionately known to his students, behind his back, as "Pop" Durst. Pop had been a journeyman machinist in industry at one time, had struggled to get a university degree and teacher training, and spent the last thirty years or so of his working life in the career that he loved, seeking to influence eager young minds in high school. Pop was a big man physically, and his imposing presence was used to assert a firm control over those under his charge. There were no discipline problems in his classes. You wouldn't want to push Pop to the place where he would need to exercise any sort of enforcement of his authority; you just did what he said. And that included, in particular, obeying the one ironclad law that was to be regarded by all as an absolutely non-negotiable regulation. The one specifically delineated commandment that Pop had set out, the one absolutely unbendable, let alone unbreakable, precept that he insisted upon, had to do with a set of six-inch steel rules that were kept in the tool crib in his shop classroom. (He insisted that these were not "rulers," as common parlance would have it, but "rules," as a good machinist would term them.) Those little rules were little gems. They were so handy, not only in shop but in geometry, in art, in drafting, and in so many other areas both at home and at school, that any boy using one in Machine Shop might just be inclined to forget to return it, and walk away with it as a piece of booty. Well, you may think so; but not a chance! Pop's law in this case was absolute. No class was ever dismissed until all the rules were accounted for and back in place in the tool crib. It didn't matter if there was another teacher waiting somewhere for a class that was going to be late. Let that teacher wait, and let that class never show up at all if that were necessary. Nobody was going anywhere out of Machine Shop until all the rules were safe. Nobody was going to smuggle contraband across the borders of Pop's classroom! And not infrequently, there would be a delay at the end of a class period, as a dozen or so boys searched high and low to discover a missing rule. And always the result was the same. The rules all showed up. Nobody ever got one out of Pop's domain. And then came the fateful day that I remember.

My class had finished their work for the day. We had all gotten cleaned up, and we were waiting for the bell and Pop's dismissal before moving on to our next class; and that's when the notice was given. "There is a rule missing! Everybody knows what that means. It has to be put back! There will be no questions asked as long as that rule is returned immediately. Do it now!" But there was no response. "Search the premises! Scour every nook and cranny! Overlook nothing!" Done; and still no rule. The bell sounds for the next class. "Stay where you are!" Pop roars. "That rule has to be returned!" Horrors! Can it be that someone is bold enough, or sly enough, or just plain stupid enough to try to flaunt Pop's authority and actually steal a rule? That must be the case. Otherwise, our meticulous search would have turned the rule up. This looks like a showdown! The wrath of Pop is about to descend on someone! That rule will be found even if it means a merciless and relentless grilling of every suspect; and every boy present is a suspect. Thus did the investigation begin, amid loud and righteous protestations on the part of each boy in turn.

"I don't know where the rule is," said one. "I had one out, but I put it back," responded another. "I know mine was returned," attested still another; and so on, right down the line to me. "Well," I offered airily, secure in the knowledge of my own innocence, "I don't have any idea where that rule is," waving my arm in a gesture of emphasis as I spoke. But behold! What is that sound of a tinkling clatter that I hear? What is that musical little noise that stills all other noises, and impinges on every ear with the ominous portent of a cannon of doom, and swings all attention to *me,* and rivets every eye directly and accusingly on *me?* It is the sound of a six-inch steel rule slipping out of the breast pocket of the smock that I had been wearing during the class, and falling to the cement floor! It is the missing rule showing up to accuse me and convict me of a flagrant breach of law and ethics! I picked the rule up and looked at it in amazement—in horrified disbelief! There was no sound from the other members of the group, but in my mind I fancied them, as they ringed me around, chanting accusingly, like a mocking Greek chorus: "Ha! There is your would-be thief, Pop! Caught red-handed! Take him, and punish him; reproach him and humiliate him; and let the rest of us go!"

As long as I live I will remember that moment and the moment that followed it. Surely, Pop would have been well within his rights to simply let justice take its course. It wasn't necessary even to bother asking me for some sort of lame excuse. It wasn't necessary even to bother reading out the charges in a voice of absolute judgment. It only remained to turn in fury to one so obviously guilty and pronounce a sentence of shame and punishment upon me.

In that setting, it seemed almost as though time stood still for one brief instant; and in that instant, before anything else could be said or done, Pop Durst and I stood face to face, looking eye to eye. Before I could blurt out my plea of "not guilty"—not even by reason of insanity!—and assure him that I was as surprised as anyone else that the rule had been in my possession; before he could bring down the gavel of condemnation, so that justice might both be done and appear to the waiting class to be done; Pop Durst made a decision and took an action based on the personhood of the boy before him. Maybe I was guilty, for all he knew. Maybe I *should* be made an example before the waiting class. But—what is the most constructive thing that could be done under the circumstances? I tell you, I think I knew in that moment just how the woman who was brought to Jesus for sentencing felt! (See John 8:1-11). The hammer was about to fall! But Pop changed all of that. Reaching out good-naturedly to tousle my hair, he simply took the rule from my trembling hand, smiled gently and understandingly, and said, "Oh well, I guess that could happen to anybody. Class dismissed!"

I recall that incident from years ago as a significant moment in my life. It was not the fact that I had been legally acquitted, that my innocence had been officially affirmed by what took place, that made the moment meaningful. It was simply that one human being, in a position to either crush or to help another human being, had chosen the more unlikely and difficult course of extending the gift of caring and helping to that other person. I was given a lift and a boost that has stayed with me as a form of encouragement for all the years that have passed since. It wasn't just that Pop believed me. It was that he believed *in* me that somehow reached down into my soul and made a difference to me. And, although that little incident in a high school shop so long ago will never be recorded in history books, and has undoubtedly long since passed from the minds of those who were there to witness it; yet I think I can actually say that I am a better person today than I might otherwise have been, simply because one decent human being cared enough about me as a person to be more interested in *helping* me than in simply letting me take my lumps. And that being the case, then surely I ought to be concerned about passing on to someone else the same kind of help that I received.

Helping Is The One Process In Which EVERYBODY WINS

Helpful actions that are extended to other persons with the anticipation or expectation of some gain or advantage are improperly motivated. No one should set about to help others under the impression that this is a paying proposition—my luck will improve, my affairs will run more smoothly, things will fall into place for me, because that will be my reward for putting myself out for someone else. It doesn't necessarily work out that way; and that is not what I mean, anyway, when I affirm that helping is a process in which everybody wins. Certainly it is to be hoped that the person being helped wins, in the sense of having some positive contribution made to his or her life. But the one who helps is also enriched—deeply and meaningfully—by the sense of having participated in the life of a fellow human traveler to the enhancement of that individual's personhood. It's doubtful that your money will be wonderfully increased if you follow the Golden Rule; and it's highly unlikely that someone will come along and do twice as much for you as you ever did for anyone else; and I doubt that fame and fortune will suddenly smile on you because you happened to do something worthy. But if your helping was really sincere, that won't matter at all. Helping is not like some tawdry chain letter, where you only put something in because you expect to get something more out! But your act of helping will return to you with a great increase of satisfaction, because your own spirit will rejoice in the simple but wonderful fact that you were able to do something constructive and beneficial for someone else. If you really want to feel good inside, try helping. It can change the situation of someone around you. It can change the temper of our society and our world. And it can change *you!* What a blessed lift it is to find that trying to add to the happiness of someone else is actually more fun than trying to grasp and embrace happiness directly for oneself! It's enough to make you want to play the role of the Good Samaritan with grateful abandon, in the sure knowledge that whatever it costs us, our return in emotional and spiritual recompense will be amply rewarding.

"Lord, help me to *help!*"

Notes

[1] Martin Buber, *Tales of the Hasidim: The Later Masters* (New York: Schocken Books, 1948) p.89.

[2] Emily Dickinson, 1830-1886, from her poem "Helpfulness."

Chapter 9 All You Have To Do Is Be *INVISIBLE*

Be careful not to do your 'acts of righteousness' before men. So when you give to the needy, do not announce it with trumpets, as the hypocrites do in the synagogues and on the streets, to be honored by men. . . . Do not let your left hand know what your right hand is doing (Matthew 6:1-3).

The above statement of Jesus employs the literary device of hyperbole—a deliberate exaggeration meant to heighten the effect of the instruction that is given. It's an exaggeration in that, of course, nobody ever really hires a brass band or engages an announcer to make sure that his or her virtuous deeds are recognized and that his or her praises are sounded before people. Jesus just talked that way to get our attention, so that we would pay heed to what He was trying to tell us; which, in our own vernacular would go something like this: "Keep a low profile as you go through life. Don't draw attention to yourself and insist that everybody ought to know about the wonderful things that you have done. Strive, in short, to be invisible."

That sounds pretty daunting—and, if the truth is told, maybe even a bit deflating. Oh, not that you or I have ever wanted to be acclaimed as the greatest thing since sliced bread! Not that we have ever wanted to have the crowd at our feet, with our special and exceptional qualities being loudly published and acknowledged. (Well, *hardly ever!)* But, nonetheless, it must be acknowledged that for most people a little praise is sweet, a little recognition is rewarding, and at the very least, a little respect is most welcome. After all, when you think of even the Lone Ranger, that self-effacing fictional hero of the Old West, you see a little bit of ego-gratification sneaking into even his low-key act. Don't you think that the Lone Ranger garnered at least a smidgen of secret pleasure from the awe-struck tone of the wonderingly thankful people whom he and Tonto had helped, when those people asked almost reverently, as the heroic duo rode away, "Who was that masked man, anyway?" Don't you think he relished those moments when all eyes were directed to him and he was affirmed as the man of the hour? And didn't you always find a note of triumph, and even a little bit of showing off, in that attention-getting and somewhat self-serving final yell of his, "Hi-yo Silver, *awa-a-a-ay*"? Well, that's not surprising. After all, what's the fun of being the Lone Ranger if you can't bask at least once in a while in the glory of the job?

Nonetheless, not that way lies the road on which we must journey towards our goal of *being* and *becoming*. Yes, there is a certain amount of satisfaction that can be obtained in the recognition of ourselves by others and the praise of our deeds and conduct. And Jesus, in the same chapter wherein we find the words that were quoted at the beginning of this consideration, acknowledged as much. There is such a thing as "the praises of people." Moreover, He affirmed, you can have that approbation and approval if you want it. But—there's just one slight hitch. If that's your choice, that's *all* you get! Maybe, on the high side of the scale, you can get yourself praised or celebrated or even idolized. Or, maybe, at the more pedestrian and common level of living where most of us find ourselves, you can at least make sure that nobody overlooks anything you've done, so that you at least get "credit where credit is due." But there's an unspoken rule of inverse rewards associated with all of that that has a great deal to do with the amount of ultimate inner satisfaction we shall really know. And it works simply like this.

The more you seek to find overt and specific recognition and approval for who you are or what you've done, and the more you get that sort of thing, the more it becomes the food on which you must feed your soul. It becomes your addiction. You need it, and you seek it out, and you literally live by it and on it. But, along with that—as a side-effect, we might say—the more you find yourself nourishing your personal Self on that kind of tangible gratification, ironically, the hungrier your true Self will grow for full and meaningful satisfaction because the less will the more profound nurture of spiritual depth and meaning find its way into your being. God's grace, and the growth-enhancing power of His presence, don't come with the feeding of the ego's pride on the praises of other persons. The deep springs of inner satisfaction that water and fructify your essential personhood can only spring up to bless and enrich your soul as the shallow desire for outward praise and commendation is relinquished.

Invisibility Is A Derivative Of Humility

Essentially, in its common biblical sense, humility simply means not thinking of yourself more highly than you ought to think (Romans 12:3). Moreover, still in terms of its biblical import, humility might also be said to mean not thinking of yourself more *often* than you ought to think. All of which, however, does not mean that one is never to derive satisfaction or a sense of accomplishment from what one has done. It simply means that the fulfillment that one realizes from having done something worthy or even noteworthy is to be found in the actual doing of it and the ensuing outcome of it, and not in any recognition or praise that might accompany it. To do good for the sake of the approval and applause of others is really only a subtle form of selfishness. Our actions are to be rendered out of our own integrity and for their own worthiness' sake.

Sometimes this is a hard thing for us to do, and not always for the worst of reasons. Sometimes our desire to be effective drives us to want to see and be assured of results, so that we may know that what we are doing is purposeful and worthwhile. Most of us find it difficult simply to tiptoe furtively through life, as it were, silently and surreptitiously, scattering our good deeds anonymously as we go. We want to see the seeds of our actions bear fruit and we want to have the gratification of knowing that what we did made a difference. Otherwise, how will we or anyone else ever know how we're doing?

Edward E. Thornton speaks pointedly to just such an issue in his book, *Theology and Pastoral Counselling.*[1] Chapter three in that book asks the pertinent question, "Who Has the Last Word?" and deals with the matter of actually knowing that we have been the means through which some good action or purpose has been realized. What a wonderful feeling it is to know that we have struck the final blow, that we have said the decisive word or done the decisive deed that actually accomplishes something worthy in life. That is having the last word in a fulfilling and effective way. But who really has that last word? And is not that last word, when it does finally get spoken, preceded by and intrinsically dependent upon other words, perhaps many in number, that have had to be previously spoken in order to lead up to and provide for that one final word? What about all those other words, and all those other deeds, that apparently were just thrown into the mix along the way? Weren't they just as critical and just as necessary as the final word and deed? Yes, of course. And someone who, somewhere away back along the trail of some individual's life said or did something helpful or encouraging or sustaining, is every bit as much a contributor to whatever outcome is realized in that individual's final experience as the one who says the word or does the action that finally brings it all to fruition. And Edward Thornton recognizes that fact in his book, and delineates the kinds of words and deeds that go to make up a whole action in the terms "ultimate" and "penultimate." "Ultimate" we know. That's the final word. That's the game-winning grand slam home run in the bottom of the ninth that clinches the pennant or wins the World Series and brings every hometown fan cheering to his or her feet. But what about the "penultimate?" Well, maybe that's no more than the routine catching of a fly ball back in the fourth inning, or the nice handling of a grounder in the sixth, neither of which appeared at the time to be spectacular but both of which, nonetheless, contributed to the progress and ultimate outcome of the game. Those actions, too, are critical, though they are not the "last word." And so it is in life. All along our way, as we meet and interact with other persons, we may be lying in wait for our chance to say to them the ultimate word or to do for them the ultimate deed, to clear the bases with one mighty, heroic swing, so to speak, and accomplish if not something spectacular then at least something significant. But: "Who hath despised the day of small things?" (Zechariah 4:10 KJV). Is it not just as vital and just as satisfying to know that even a small, admittedly penultimate word or deed that I have offered has played a critical part in the overall scheme, even though my name won't be the one in the headlines on tomorrow's sports page? So Thornton observes: "The penultimate includes all the things that aid in providing the route over which God travels in coming to (persons)." [2]

In the light of that it is no insignificant thing, then, to be involved in the saying and doing of the penultimate! By willingly acting out of a humility that does not demand star billing, we can actually be links in the chain whereby God reaches out to touch and help another person. So what if our action is no more than "a cup of cold water" (Matthew 10:42)! It is our part to give that cup of cold water as a genuine act of ministry, not only as *all* that we *can* do but as *the least* that we are *willing* to do. And who knows just where that might fit in as part of God's granting of His grace within any given situation? Thornton adds something else:

> No one has the last word; yet everyone may have the next to the last word. . . . Although no one form of ministry is in itself ultimate, all forms of ministry may be penultimate.[3]

That makes the deliberate practice of being invisible both more practical and more exciting! Who knows but that in simply being willing to do what I can, where and when I can, without worrying about whether it will be worthwhile enough to be noticed or applauded, I may actually do something that forwards the work of God and brings the grace of God into another person's experience; that I may actually help to "prepare the way of the Lord" by contributing to the chain of events that God uses in coming to another person? That kind of reflection could almost be enough to encourage humility as a way of life!

"Seekest thou great things for thyself? Seek them not" (Jeremiah 45:5 KJV). Humility is willing to take the lower place in order that the greater good may come about.

I remember reading years ago a story about two young men from North America who were traveling through Britain shortly after World War II and who came, on their journey, to spend a night at Oxford University. It was during the summertime, when classes were out and accommodation was available in a number of the colleges there; and these two were happy to be able to bunk down in such a famous school. Their delight was even further increased when, as they registered, the porter who was checking them in observed the number of the room that they had been assigned, and commented, "Why, that's the same room that Mahatma Gandhi slept in when he was here last year." What a thrill! They were going to stay in the same quarters as such a great and famous man! That would give them something to talk about when they got back home! They went to the room, looked at its arrangement, and realized immediately that they had a problem. There were two single beds, one against either wall of the room. How could they possibly know in which bed Gandhi had actually slept? How were they ever going to be able to brag to their friends, "I slept exactly where Gandhi slept?" But they did not trouble themselves for long. They hit upon the perfect solution. Each of them would just turn in in one of the beds, retiring at eleven o'clock. They would set the alarm clock for three a.m., at which time they would get up, switch the blankets and trade places, with each then sleeping in the other bed until seven in the morning. Then, when they got up, they could both claim that they had slept in the bed where Gandhi had slept. They congratulated themselves on their ingenuity, and put their strategy into effect accordingly. It went off without a hitch; and the next morning, as they were checking out after breakfast, they told the porter of their scheme and they couldn't help bragging just a little bit about how they had carried it out. The porter, however, had one final bit of information to impart to them. "When Mr. Gandhi was here," he said, "he slept on the floor!"

Invisibility Does Not Mean That I Am A Nonentity

It needs to be understood that invisibility does not mean the practice of being simply self-deprecating or self-minimizing. It does not mean putting yourself down and losing the significance of your own being. Certainly it does mean the opposite of being self-promoting and self-aggrandizing, but only because the person striving for invisibility is confident enough and assured enough in his or her own sense of personal identity not to need the false security, and not to desire the shallow praise, that may be found in grabbing after approbation and accolades. One's own legitimate sense of personal dignity and worth is neither established nor disestablished by the presence or absence of the limelight. That involves a different kind of light, as the following may illustrate.

When I was a teenager, attending worship in my home church, we had a pastor who carried out one part of the service in exactly the same way literally every week. I don't believe that I ever heard him vary this particular part of our worship even once over the entire period of the several years that he served in our midst. It was always the same. Whenever he would prepare to announce the offering, he would do so with the one offertory sentence that is forever stuck in my mind: "Let your light so shine before men that they may see your good works and glorify your Father who is in heaven" (Matthew 5:16 KJV).

For many years, when I was quite young, I thought that that verse referred simply to our giving of our offerings in order to show our love for God. Then, as I grew older and gained some further understanding of the Christian faith, I came to believe that it meant even more than that. I came to see and understand that it had something to do with "witnessing." I understood it to mean that I ought to be prepared to show forth the convictions of my faith in all settings, regardless of where I was or whom I was with, in the spirit of the Sunday School song, "This little light of mine, I'm gonna let it shine, let it shine, let it shine, let it shine."

But I think now that there is an even richer dimension to those words of Jesus—a dimension related directly to our quest to *be* and to *become*. I believe now that Jesus was speaking not just commandingly about giving and witnessing, but also encouragingly and helpfully about being one's own true self and simply letting your own essential personhood shine or radiate forth in everything you do and are. And if that is the case, then Jesus is certainly not asking us to adopt a false diffidence or to labor under a painful putting down of our best selves. That would be to hide our light under a bushel! Rather, let it shine! Thank God for the gift of your life and your person, thank Him for the journey of discovery towards *being* and *becoming* that He has started you on; and strive to live up to the highest level of personhood of which you are capable. You can be truly humble and confidently *invisible* as you do that, because you have an inner strength that allows you to be yourself with everything you've got while not requiring that others substantiate or validate your own deepest sense of who you are by the grace of God.

Invisibility Is A Path To Spirituality

Jesus' dictum, "Whoever tries to keep his life will lose it, and whoever loses his life will preserve it (Luke 17:33), sets out the basis for our aspiring to invisibility. Losing one's life, in the sense in which Jesus spoke here, certainly involves being willing to live invisibly; whereas, high visibility, in the sense of straining after conspicuousness, and determining not to be overlooked, is certainly an effort towards "saving" one's life—assiduously asserting one's reputation and standing. But again, the deepest consequences are actually ironically inverse. The one who insists on living visibly eventually ends up with a shallow, unsatisfying emptiness of person and soul, with nothing truly worthwhile to show for it; while the one who is content to humble himself or herself will be "exalted" (see Matthew 23:12)—exalted, that is, to a place of soul-enriching and person-satisfying fellowship with God. So the secret is to embrace the concept of willing invisibility, of willing readiness to "lose one's life," so that we come ultimately to embrace the formula enunciated centuries ago by St. Augustine: "To my God, a heart of flame; to others, a heart of love; to myself, a heart of steel." It takes a great deal of resolution to be able to say and mean those beautiful words.

Oh, by the way—seen any *invisible* people lately?

Notes

1 Edward Thornton, *Theology and Pastoral Counseling* (Philadelphia: Fortress Press, 1964)

2 *ibid*, p.40.

3 *ibid.* p.41.

Chapter 10
All You Have To Do Is Be

JUST

What does the Lord require of you, but to act justly, and to love mercy, and to walk humbly with your God? (Micah 6:8).

Notice the order in which the three key elements enunciated in the preceding verse are presented to us. Even before the essentials of being merciful and reverent are declared, another element is set before us. What is required, primarily and principally, Micah says, is that we aspire to be *just.*

To Be Just Is More Than A Matter Of Mere Legalism

Too often, I think, we seem to assume that being just means no more than simply meeting the minimum legal or moral requirements that are laid upon us—so that, on the one hand, we do not step beyond the line of what is *permitted,* while, on the other hand, we do not fail to measure up to the standard of what *is required.* Accordingly, I can be depended on not to *take* anything—money, privilege, liberty, advantage—to which I am not rightly *entitled;* and not to *withhold* anything—commitment, responsibility, duty, co-operation—for which I am rightly *obligated.* Such a definition is good, but it is also, unfortunately, cold and impersonal, as formal definitions often tend to be. It does not encompass all that it can mean to be truly and fully *just,* in that it is too blatantly forensic in its nature and tends to deal essentially with abstract principles and legal niceties. Moreover, while it sets out the parameters of what is allowable or exactable, it also includes the possibility of loopholes or fine print which are entirely within the scope of literal justice but which do not take into account the spiritual nature of our living. Thus, it is possible for one person, even while adhering to the canons of legitimacy, to hurt another person, or to profit to the disadvantage or loss of that other person, or to exact crushing payment or service from him or her. And the big problem with all of that is that, while such approaches may be *legally just*, and nothing *less*, they can also be *just legal*, and nothing *more*; as the following may illustrate.

There was once a certain investor who was on a trip out of the country, in a hard to reach spot, who received an urgent cablegram from his wife. It seems that a business associate had made a very lucrative offer on some obscure gold mine stocks that the investor had had lying around for years—a very forgettable, not to say regrettable investment concerning which he had given up all hope of ever recouping even his original outlay. As far as he was concerned they weren't even worth the paper they were printed on. Imagine his surprise, then, to receive the cable from his wife advising him, "Jones wants to buy gold stock. He offers one hundred dollars per share." Elated, the man cabled back an immediate return, "Sell! Stocks are in upstairs safe." Before long, however, another urgent communication came from the wife: "Can't get the safe open." To which the man instantly replied with the fervent instructions, "Throw in the safe!"

One could make a number of observations about the attitude displayed in that exchange of cablegrams. You could say it was sharp, or shrewd. It may be described as opportunistic and maybe selfish. But . . . could you call it unjust? Maybe not technically; but it certainly needs some looking at in terms of its being a basic principle of human interaction and a basic principle of worthy human becoming.

Being Just Is An Acknowledgement Of Inter-Relatedness

I remember from my very early years a song of the sort that used to get sung at community gatherings, along with such perennial favorites as "My Wild Irish Rose," "A Bicycle Built For Two," and the like. This one was the old rouser, "Hail, Hail the Gang's All Here;" and as I reflect on it now it occurs to me that it contained one of the most unjust sentiments I have ever heard expressed. Of course, the song was light-hearted in the extreme, and it was never intended that anyone should form a code of conduct for life based on its sentiments; but it nonetheless appeared to my impressionable mind to be making a statement of philosophy that had to be understood in reverse if the camaraderie of the lyrics was to be realized in truth. I am thinking of the line that said rather raucously, "What the heck do we care, as long as we get our share!" I am certain that, over the years, those words have been sung with gusto by almost countless numbers of people who, in their hearts, really felt and believed quite otherwise. And quite otherwise is how it must be for the person who seeks, in his or her doings, to be just. It is impossible to live justly if one's basic orientation is one that dictates, "The best deal for me, and good luck to anybody else involved." That philosophy fails to grasp the realization that there can be no true justice that is not justice for all concerned. And that principle reaches out beyond merely financial considerations to embrace and involve all areas of our lives.

Let me bring this aspect of our understanding into clearer focus by telling you of an example of its direct opposite.

I do not have many cut-and-dried routines in my life, but I do have one procedure that I that I follow almost without fail on the first Monday of every month with regard to my banking needs. Each month, on that appointed day, I get into my car, drive down to the business section of the city where I live, park in the municipal parking lot, and walk two blocks down the main street to my bank. There I may make various deposits or withdrawals, or simply handle other business which I feel requires a living teller rather than an automated one, after which I walk back the two blocks to where I have parked. I've been doing that for a number of years, and it is a very routine and ordinary experience for me—usually. Nothing much ever happens, and I make my little journey without incident—usually. But one day, something did occur that was out of the ordinary and that taught me something about human nature.

It was a Monday morning much like any other Monday morning, you might say. I was part way through my routine, having arrived downtown, parked, made my trek to the bank, put my financial affairs in order there, and started my return walk to my car. As I was making my way back along the street towards where I had parked, I casually observed the people around me. This was a bright September day, with the tang of fall in the air, when it felt good to be outside; and consequently there were quite a number of people about, although the sidewalk was hardly crowded. I was enjoying watching people who were themselves enjoying the day, when my eye was caught by the figure of a young man who was walking perhaps ten or twelve feet in front of me, going in the same direction that I was going. I never did see his face, since his back was of course to me, but I got a pretty good idea of what he was like. He was fairly tall, just about six feet, I judged, with light blond curly hair that came down to and spilled over the collar of the denim jacket that he was wearing. He had on blue jeans and some sort of gym shoes, and his shoulders were broad and square. I remember the shoulders particularly—and you'll see why in just a moment.

He was making his way along among the other pedestrians when I happened to look beyond him to the flow of persons ahead, where I saw another young man walking in the oncoming direction towards us. I could see that this young man, too, was fairly tall, just about six feet, and that he also had longish hair that came down to and over his collar. There were two differences, though, between the two young men, that I observed immediately. One difference, which was totally irrelevant but which I simply noted in passing, was that the oncoming man's hair was black and straight, and not blond and curly; and the other difference, which was much more significant, was that he was obviously blind, since he was tapping and feeling the way ahead of him with a long white cane as he walked.

I had hardly had time to notice these things when I observed something else. The young blond man, who had to this point been walking normally to one side in order to accommodate oncomers, suddenly veered in his progress and began walking out of his way to bring himself directly into the path of the other young man as he approached. The second man, of course, being blind, had no knowledge of this. As the two men neared each other, it was obvious to me that there was going to be a collision unless the sighted man changed his course. He didn't. Instead, just as he drew up to where the blind man was, he hunched his big shoulders up like a hockey player about to dish out a body-check, dipped himself to one side, and slammed himself into the chest of the oncoming man. Then he gave himself a sort of satisfied hitch, and continued arrogantly and uncaringly on his way. I was shocked. That this had been a deliberately intended offensive move was beyond doubt. And I was infuriated to the point of outrage by what I had seen—so much so that, just for an instant, I thought of sprinting ahead to catch up to the young blond man, to confront him and rebuke him over what he had done, and maybe even give him a taste of his own medicine! But—that was just for an instant. I immediately re-evaluated the wisdom of such a course. I had a vision of what might well result from such an action on my part—namely, our city newspaper featuring an article with the headline: "Local Clergyman in Jail for Assault and Battery, and Disturbing the Peace." (Or, perhaps more *realistically,* "Local Clergyman in *Hospital,* with *Broken Bones,* and *Severe Multiple Contusions!")* At any rate, I was stopped in my foolhardy inclination, as much by the young blind man as by anything else. I looked at him to observe his actions after he had been struck.

At first there was a look of astonishment and perplexity on his face. You could tell that he literally didn't know what had hit him. Moreover, he had no idea if there was more of the same yet to come. He was, understandably, momentarily shaken and disoriented. But this quickly passed. When no further attack was forthcoming, and it seemed that the incident was over, this young man simply gathered himself together, reached out his cane again before him, and began calmly and even serenely, I thought, to continue on his way. And as he passed me, he was the picture of composure and dignity, walking slowly but firmly, with a slight smile of well-being on his face.

What came to my mind then was a verse of scripture from Matthew's Gospel, where Jesus made the pronouncement, "If your right eye causes you to sin, gouge it out and throw it away. It is better for you to lose one part of your body than for your whole body to go into hell" (Matthew 5:29). And what I thought in this regard was that, indeed, I would rather be blind, as the dark-haired young man was, and be able to live with dignity and integrity as he had shown that he could do, than to possess my eyesight and act as despicably and contemptibly and as *unjustly* as had the other young man! I would rather be sightless than, seeing, to live so hellishly! In short, I would rather be the blind man than the blond man! And then, immediately, I had to check myself on that sentiment, to ask myself if that was all rhetoric or if I really meant that heated observation. After all, that was not something to be expressed lightly. Which led to a further realization that made those almost fierce words of Jesus very applicable to me. I don't have to make my response to the declaration of Jesus an either/or thing. I have my eyesight, and am free to choose how I shall employ it. I can act selfishly and cruelly as a sighted person; or I can act with honor and virtue as a sighted person. Seeing or not seeing is not the key. My young blind friend's dignity and composure were not related simply to his sightlessness, but to his character. And what was of vital significance in the exchange that had taken place between the two young men was not who could or could not see what was going on but, rather, simply what was going on itself! One individual was taking cruel and shoddy advantage over another individual just because he could. And that unfair situation, and not any particular virtue on my part, was what led me to be upset at the whole affair. As well it should; indeed, as well it *must!* How can I or anyone else feel that life is what it should be if acts of injustice are being committed against other persons? How can I or anyone else be bettered or enriched through the loss or hurt of another person? "'Each for himself,' said the elephant, as he danced among the chickens," cannot be an acceptable understanding of our relation to one another.

Being Just Is The Outward Expression Of An Inward Persuasion

Why be just at all? Why worry about the welfare of someone else beyond the bare legal requirements of not overstepping, or falling short of, the stated demands of the law? Is it because someone might catch me at it? Is it because I might be reprimanded or punished? Is it because, if I am unjust to someone, someone else may be even more unjust to me? The questions are all academic, of course, because my concern to be a just person does not arise from any such considerations, practical or philosophical. Rather, there is a much more profound and primary principle at work. It is the one expressed in the scriptural declaration, "This is (God's) command: to believe in the name of His Son, Jesus Christ, and to love one another" (1 John 3:23). Love, we are told, does two things. First, it "does no wrong to its neighbor," and is therefore "the fulfillment of the law;" and, second, it "is not self-seeking," with each person looking not only at his or her own interests, but "also to the interests of others" (Romans 13:10, 1 Corinthians 13:5, Philippians 2:4). And to say that we believe in Jesus; to confess Him as Lord and Savior, and strive to follow in His way; is naturally to be impelled to express, then, in His name, what we might simply call "love in its working clothes," which is *justice*—hearty, helpful, and humane. This comes about according as we are moved by an inner reality that says "I do this not because I *have* to, nor really even because I *ought* to; but rather, I do this because, in my best and most aware and most truly human moments, I *want* to."

Some years ago, when our children were small, I learned a lesson in inner motivation and the conscientious expression of self when I helped one of our youngsters look for some item in a toy-box. I forget what we were seeking at the time, but I have never forgotten our incidental discovery of something else. Tucked away, deep down in one corner of the box, where it had been out of sight and out of mind for who knows how long, lying forgotten and unnoticed in the darkness, we came across a toy compass. That instrument had, of course, been designed to point always to the North Pole. After all, even though it was just a toy, it was endued with the magnetic qualities that caused it to show true north and that could, in a critical situation, actually be the means of saving lives. But it had been set aside and neglected for an indefinite period. No inquiring childish eye had sought it out. No eager young hand had reached for it. And under those circumstances, if it were human, who could have blamed it for "turning off" for a while, for slackening its unbending proclivity to keep pointing to the north? Who would ever know the difference? What was it going to matter, or what was it going to hurt, if the compass relaxed and pointed east, west, or south, or even spun around carelessly at its own inclination? But of course it did not do that. And I was struck by the obvious object lesson that lay before us as we found that compass. It was still pointing north when we discovered it, just as it had continued to point north all the while when no one had known or cared. It did so simply because its own magnetized needle was drawn to, and compelled by, a mighty force beyond itself, the great magnetic pole towards which it was unalterably oriented.

Maybe at times I find myself to be just about like that toy compass—in a situation where nobody ever either could or would be checking up on me. But, because of the compulsive pull of God's grace upon me, I nonetheless want to be just in all things and towards all persons. This is to aspire to a goal that is in itself a most worthy polestar for human action. It is to seek after being a part of that company described by one New Testament writer as follows:

> Ye are come . . . unto the city of the living God, . . . to the general assembly and Church of the Firstborn, which are written in heaven; and to God, the Judge of all men; and to the spirits of *just* (persons) made perfect (Hebrews 12:22-23 KJV).

Chapter 11
All You Have To Do Is Be
KIND

"Love is kind" (1 Corinthians 13:4).

Why are people often so skin-flinty with *kindness?* Why does it appear so often to be such a rare and meagerly distributed commodity in our world, when its power for good and blessing is so obvious and beneficial? Such a state of scantiness, where it exists, is serious, sad, and even sinful, and cries out to be corrected.

There Is AFFIRMATION In Being Kind

One of the most generous and constructive features of Jesus' dealings with persons was His attitude of receptiveness and approval. Oh, Jesus could be, and was, as the occasion required, both confronting and challenging. He was no easy mark or simple pushover for con artists or deceivers. He unerringly saw through pretense and insincerity, and unhesitatingly shattered pomposity and hypocrisy. But His basic and constant attitude was one of kindness and encouragement.

The Apostle John tells, in chapter three of his Gospel, the significant story of how one particular person, a Pharisee named Nicodemus, came to Jesus by night seeking an audience. Nicodemus came as a seeker after ultimate truth. He came with a determined purpose. He came with urgency and intensity. He came with a question. Observe how he was received and treated.

Note first of all that Jesus was both addressable and courteous. There was no brusqueness, no condescension, and certainly no underlying impatience or irritability in His manner, no hidden message that He really had better things to do than devote his time to some uninvited interloper. I believe that Nicodemus felt that Jesus was genuinely interested in him and concerned for his welfare. It is interesting that Jesus is sometimes spoken of as having a "therapeutic personality." His very presence was healing and assuring. Just to be near Him was to feel an uplifting, cleansing, strengthening influence that pointed you towards God and purity and worthy living. And integral to that whole impact of Jesus' person and personality was His gracious manner of *kindness*. He never stinted with that.

And note further that Jesus' kindness and His affirmation were constructive in nature. He wasn't just trying to be a nice guy, coming on all mushy and gushy. That sort of thing may be artificially attractive at first, but it tends to cloy, and wear thin after a while. Rather, Jesus was trying to provide a helpful and liberating and even empowering experience for this seeking one. And He was doing this by trying to impart to Nicodemus a sublime and transcendent truth. He was trying to show Nicodemus that he could receive the gift of eternal life from God. So Nicodemus was affirmed not only by a presence but also by a pronouncement. "This Life comes to you," Jesus declared, "as you are born *from above.*" And I italicize that expression deliberately, because the words used there pinpoint so emphatically the truth that Jesus was trying to share, namely: "You are made new and alive through this gift from *God, above.*" Which, one might think, seems very simple and straightforward. As we might say today, "What part of 'from above' don't you understand?" But Nicodemus, despite what we might see as the clarity of our Lord's teaching, had some trouble with what Jesus was saying. He missed the essential thrust of our Lord's words, and got a slightly twisted perception of their meaning.

The problem is that the word we find in the New Testament that means "from above," is the same word that can also, when the context warrants it, be translated to mean "again;" and that's where Nicodemus took the wrong fork in the road. He misconstrued the words of Jesus and gave them a very limited meaning, taking Jesus to have said simply, "You must be born *again*"—(literally, "one more time.") Well, yes, it *is* being born "again," of course, in that a birth from above is a "second" birth, secondary to our having been born in the natural sense in the first place; but the primary significance of this birth has to do not with its *incidental numerality* but with its *marvelous originating source.* It is not just being born again, as factual as that may be; it is being born again *from above,* as essential and life giving as that is. Nicodemus, however, failed to grasp that; and so he stumbled along in his conversation with Jesus on a distressingly literal level, prompting him, then, to ask a very famous question.

You know how most of us hesitate to ask questions, sometimes, because we don't want to appear to be "dumb"? Well, part of kindness, surely, is the receiving and fielding of such questions. We've all had teachers or professors who have told us something like, "Don't be afraid to ask any question that you have. Don't keep quiet through shyness or embarrassment. If you want to know something, ask. Probably somebody else is sitting there wanting to ask the very same thing. There are no dumb questions." And sometimes we have been reassured through the kindness of such words to ask what we might otherwise have kept to ourselves. Well, Jesus was kind, and Nicodemus sensed that. So he asked his question. And it should be of great consolation to all the rest of us that it turned out to be probably the single dumbest question of all time! What Nicodemus asked reminds me, in essence, of the antics of Barney Rubble in the old Flintstones cartoons. Sometimes—perhaps, for example, when Fred was trying to outline some plan, or provide some sort of explanation—Barney would become confused and would fail to grasp things clearly; and he would show his confusion by blinking his big, round eyes, shaking his head vaguely from side to side, and saying in puzzlement, "Duhhh, I don't get it, Fred!" Quite frankly, Nicodemus might just as well have said, *"Duhhh, I don't get it, Jesus!"*

"You must be born from above," Jesus declared. And Nicodemus could only perceive within those words that level of communication that said, "You must be born again." So that's when he asked his question—the world's blue-ribbon, record-holding, gold-plated, dumbest question ever asked: "Do you mean I have to somehow get back into my mother's body again, and be born one more time?"

Jesus could have responded in one of several ways at that point. For one thing, our Lord could have cut Nicodemus *off,* in exasperation. "This guy's hopeless," Jesus might have thought. "Why should I waste My time on him?" Or, Jesus could have cut Nicodemus *down,* with criticism. "Here's an 'F' on your paper on spiritual perception. Go to the bottom of the class!" Or, further still, Jesus might have cut Nicodemus *up,* with sarcasm. "Yes," He might have replied to Nicodemus's inane inquiry, "And this time make sure that you get a brain before you make your appearance!" But everything that I know about Jesus tells me that, because of His kindness, He *would* not and indeed He surely *could* not have made such remarks. But, alas, some of His followers have been known to do just that sort of thing when faced with exasperating or trying circumstances in dealing with other persons. At work, at home, at play—anywhere and everywhere where human interactions test our patience and forbearance, where people "rub us the wrong way," and push our tolerance to the limit, what is our response to these "burrs under our saddle"? Ah, too often anger, arrogance, gruffness and impatience have been the attitudes reflected in dealing with difficult individuals, and the *kindness* of consideration and forbearance has been conspicuously absent. And thereby some who have even desired to experience and reflect the best qualities of a full-orbed personhood have lost an opportunity to do two things. They have lost the chance to uplift and affirm another person and help that person towards being freed for personal becoming. And they have lost an opportunity that might have allowed them to become more like Jesus in being a helpful and constructive person in their own right. Jesus did not simply write Nicodemus off and send him away, with a sad shake of the head and a fervent hope that the next person who showed up would be somewhat brighter and more spiritually alert. Rather, He went on to work understandingly with Nicodemus in order to teach him—and us, through our reading of the story—the life-renewing truth we all need to know.

There Is GENEROSITY In Being Kind

Years ago, when I was in high school, our English teacher, Miss Cole, set out for our class a particular exercise having to do with a fragment of poetry that she provided. What she did was to give us a couple of lines that she said she wanted us to identify in their context—which context she professed not to know. Our assignment was to find the source from which those words were taken and bring a copy of the poem to class. (What I think now is that she simply wanted her students to go out and read through a lot of poetry—any poetry, just so long as they were searching it as they read!) No one in the class ever did find the source of our quote—which, as I was to discover only some years later was from Bliss Carman's poem, "The World at St. Kavin's"—and once the assignment concerning it was finished, all interest seemed simply to fade away for most of the class. But that "teaser" that she gave us has remained in my mind over all the intervening years; and who knows, maybe that's what Miss Cole had hoped for all along. It goes as follows:

> And I share my crust, as common manhood must,
> With one whose need is greater than my own.

That, I believe, is the philosophy of kindness. It embodies the element of generosity. It expresses care both about another person and for another person; and it affirms my readiness to give in order that another person might be helped and blessed. To do that, consistently, generously and instinctively is, as they say, a tall order. But how gracious and admirable it is to see it actually put into practice.

A friend of mine who is a minister once related to me a childhood adventure of his that may be noted here. My friend is himself the son of a minister, and was literally "raised in church," back in the years before nursery and junior congregation were such an established part of our worship patterns as they are today. In those days, for better or for worse, especially in smaller congregations, everybody was in church for the whole service. In that setting, my friend tells of something that happened to him while he was still a babe in arms, something that he does not recall personally but that was told to him by his mother, for whom it was a trying experience. (It couldn't have been any fun for the infant, either, as you'll see.)

My friend's mother, the pastor's wife, was an accomplished soprano soloist, and she was frequently asked to provide the "special music" in the services. When she was so enlisted, she would not sit in the choir loft, but simply remain in her seat near the front of the church and move to the platform when it was time for her to sing. At that point she would simply turn and hand the baby she had been holding—my friend, as an infant—to one of the ladies nearby, and that lady would tend the child until his mother returned to her seat. It was considered quite a privilege to hold the minister's baby while the minister's wife sang, and there were always eager volunteers ready to accept the tender package from the mother's arms as she would hand him over—so much so that one day a rather unusual situation developed. As the minister's wife rose to sing, she turned, as was her custom, to give her child to a willing helper, when two such willing helpers reached out their arms simultaneously, and each laid hold on some part of the baby. And then ensued a singular scene. Each lady was determined to take to herself the honor and the privilege of minding the minister's offspring! Thus, as the minister's wife proceeded to the platform to prepare herself to sing, a real tug-of-war began in the pew behind her. "*Give me that baby*!" one of the helpful parishioners fairly snarled, giving a mighty pull on her half of the unfortunate infant. "*Let go of that kid!*" the other solicitous soul raged just as savagely, yanking on her end of the child. (Shades of Solomon and his affair of the disputed baby in 1 Kings, chapter 3!) Well, so it continued in church that morning, with each of the would-be mother substitutes hauling and heaving on the helpless person of the contested infant, until one of the disputants finally gave a mighty pull and a clever twist at the same time and succeeded in wrenching the hapless infant free from her opponent's clutches. Then, clasping her prize to her bosom, the victor turned triumphantly to be seated, while her defeated foe slumped disconsolately down into her pew. It hardly needs to be said that from that day on, my friend's mother made specific arrangements ahead of time as to who would hold her child when thereafter she had to relinquish him in order to sing! But it does need to be said that what all of that taught my friend, as he heard that story and reflected on it in later years, was something about *kindness* and the lack thereof. Generosity towards another person might have moved either of those ladies to defer to the other when it became apparent that there was one pair of willing hands too many available for the coveted chore of baby-keeping. But beyond that, generosity towards the baby himself would have placed his interests and safety above the rather selfish objective of just wanting to be the favored one who got the minister's baby to hold and to tend. Fortunately, my friend came out of that escapade in one piece. But ever after he was ruefully aware of how close he had come to actually being torn limb from limb; to actually having it said that he had been killed with anything but *kindness*!

There Is GRACE In Being Kind

In our world today there are many, many persons whose lives cry out for the gift of kindness. I sometimes wonder, even as I simply walk down the crowded sidewalks of the city, how many persons whose lives thus happen to touch mine even glancingly, would, if they had the opportunity, open up and tell me that of all the things they need in life the one thing that they seek more than any other is the simple gift of a kind look, a kind word, a kind attitude. Many, many people, even in the midst of comfort and comparative affluence, are inwardly hurting. They are cut off from the deepest springs of true fulfillment and joy, and yearn for some expression of grace that can touch them and heal them and satisfy them at the most secret and profound level of their being.

One of the most appealing characters in the Bible has always been, for me, Barnabas, the sometime companion of Paul in the New Testament. He has always impressed me as being gracious, generous, approachable and accepting. He never comes across as being harsh, or curt, or judgmental or mean. His actions show him to be consistently constructive and conciliatory. The one word that jumps to my mind to define him is the beautiful word which we are now considering. I would simply describe him as *kind*. We see that this is so in the mediating role that he is seen as playing in at least three instances in the book of Acts.

At the very outset of Paul's ministry, following his Damascus-Road conversion, he sought to join himself to the disciples of Jesus, to be a part of their number. But the disciples would have nothing to do with him because of his prior record of hatred and persecution. It was only when Barnabas took it upon himself to intercede for Paul that he was able to open up the way for Paul to be accepted and welcomed, and to become the great emissary for God that he then went on to become (Acts 9:26-30).

Then there is the assignment that Barnabas was given by the Church to visit and assess and instruct the newly-organized fellowship of believers in Antioch (Acts 11:19-24). Doubtless be could have come to that setting to confront these neophyte believers with a magisterial and even dictatorial attitude, laying down the law, and squelching any methods or expressions that were not according to specific apostolic directive. He could have "rapped some knuckles" and bossed the congregation into a strict conformity. (One wonders how a hotheaded Peter or an acerbic Paul might have approached the same assignment!) But Barnabas, we are told, was simply true to his name. That name means "son of *encouragement*"—or, as the KJV has it, "son of *consolation*"—one who builds up and sustains, one who focuses on and supports that which is worthy and honorable, downplaying the inferior; in short, one who pulls the positive out of the mix and tactfully minimizes the negative so that the end result is enheartening and even ennobling. "Barnabas was a good man, full of the Holy Spirit and faith"(Acts 11:24). I find it easy to add to that description the further simple notation, "Barnabas was a *kind* man;" a third indication of which is found in his ministry to John Mark.

John Mark had apparently "flunked" his assignment as an assistant to Paul and Barnabas in their missionary work in Asia Minor, so much so that Paul dismissed him, virtually "firing" him. That literally meant the end of John Mark's usefulness as a Christian minister, unless he and his service could somehow be salvaged. Out of that situation, Paul chose sternly, and almost callously, to "cut his losses" with Mark and move on in another direction with another partner, Silas; while Barnabas, in a characteristically solicitous action, deliberately took young John Mark under his wing, offering him encouragement and support so that the tragedy of his defection was averted and he was eventually restored to an honorable ministry, even to the point of being specifically commended by Paul (Acts 16:36-41; and compare 2 Timothy 4:11).

In the light of all of which, what more is there to be said than simply: Go and do likewise: "Be *kind* to one another" (Ephesians 4:32.)

Chapter 12
All You Have To Do Is Be
LEANING

At first glance, the action of *leaning* may seem to be an expression of weakness and dependence, calling to mind the negative images of spiritual crutches or perpetual spiritual training wheels! Truly understood, however, leaning, is not at all inimical to full and independent self-reliance and self-determination. In fact, it is both supportive of, and contributive to, the spirit of self-discovery and self-direction.

St. Paul sets out the relevant principle here for us in a plain and direct statement in Philippians 2:12-13. "Work out your salvation," he enjoins first of all, bluntly and unmistakably. What could be plainer? "Roll up your sleeves and get busy at your God-given task of *becoming!*" We are to assume responsibility for our own wholeness and fullness, puzzle out and pursue our own way, encounter and overcome our own hazards, make our own choices, and win through to our own reward. But there is more, as Paul continues. "Work out your own salvation," he says; with this proviso: remembering that "it is *God who works in you,*" inwardly leading you and urging you "to will and to act according to His good purpose." Paradoxically, it seems that, on the one hand we are "on our own" in our pursuit of the prize of fullness of life, needing to work out our own way every inch of our journey by the employment of all our own faculties; while, on the other hand we are not *simply* on our own because, simultaneously, we are being led and empowered by the God who created us and endowed us with those marvelously efficient and sufficient faculties.

"Take My yoke upon you, and learn from Me, . . . and you will find rest for your souls," Jesus said (Matthew 11:28). That's encouraging, because, remember, if we are sharing Christ's yoke, then *He* is sharing *ours,* and we can lean into that yoke to draw on the resources that He is bringing to the situation.

Leaning Equips Us With God's Own Might

It makes sense to employ the fullest measure of assistance available to us in the most practical and mundane affairs of life—books for a scholar, a sword for a swordsman, operating instruments for a surgeon. Should it not also make sense to employ the best resources available to us in our quest for full personhood? I think so! And the greatest resource available to us in this regard is nothing less than the focused presence and strength of God Himself infusing us and enabling us on our onward journey. We derive the fullest richness and competency of personhood through the deep resources of spirit that are ours through our relationship with and our dependence upon God. It is as though we all stand with the woman of Samaria at the well with Jesus, beseeching Him, as she did, to give to us the Water of Life that will meet the deepest thirst of our being (see John 4:4-15).

We can haughtily refuse to draw any sustenance or refreshment from that infinite wellspring that our Lord offers; or we can wisely choose to receive from its reservoir of grace those features of insight, direction, perseverance and fulfillment that are ours for the taking. We can, in other words, come to *lean* on our Lord. And being thus related to Him, we then realize further the empowering quality that is imparted to us in our daily living. "I can do everything through Him who gives me strength," St. Paul exulted (Philippians 4:13), by which he means to assert, "I am steadied and upheld and galvanized by my reliance on Jesus my Lord."

That term "galvanized" in particular prompts an illustrative reflection, making me think of something that is said to have happened in connection with a certain family's dog after that family moved into a newly constructed house. It seems that after all the necessary hookups had been made and all the services connected to the new residence, everything worked just fine—except the telephone. It had become the source of some considerable frustration and consternation. "It isn't as though we're not receiving anything," the lady of the house said, when a repairman was dispatched. "I know that it's working to at least some degree because, believe it or not, our dog can hear it! It must be sending out one of those high-pitched signals that human ears can't pick up but that the dog can, because on certain occasions he will start to bark with extreme excitement and intensity and run and jump along the length of his chain. And then, if I pick up the receiver at that time, sure enough, there is someone on the line trying to get through to me." Well, that was a puzzling situation that the telephone company had to address; and after some considerable testing and investigation, they came up with an explanation. It seems that what was happening was this. The family dog was tied out in the back yard by means of a long chain that was fastened to his metal-studded collar at one end and attached to a metal stake driven into the ground near his kennel at the other end. Quite by accident, however, and in fact surely by the strangest of coincidences, the metal stake had been driven into the ground directly over the spot where the underground telephone cable was laid between the service post and the house. The stake actually went down far enough and directly enough to pierce the insulated sheathe on the cable and establish a short circuit in any incoming telephone signal. Thus, when the dog barked and jumped in his agitated manner, it was not because he was hearing a high-pitched sound, but because he was taking a concentrated electrical charge that jolted and activated him. Talk about a secret source of galvanic power! That dog was certainly in touch with a dynamic force that awakened and enlivened him!

Well, I certainly would not liken our sharing in the empowering life of the Spirit to that illustration on a literal basis! But the underlying—(no pun intended)—principle is valid. There is a deep and vivifying current of life that we receive and are affected by because we are open to it and seek it as a gift and a grace bestowed by our Lord. And that gift of grace truly makes an animating and empowering difference in us and to us! Thus St. Paul offers a wise and hopeful prayer for those seeking to express Christian maturity: "I pray that out of His glorious riches, (God) may strengthen you with power through His Spirit in your inner being" (Ephesians 3:16).

Leaning Keeps Us Walking Upright

Now, there's a contradiction in terms if ever there was one—and we might be inclined to retort, "Make up your mind! Either we are vertical, or we are on an angle; either we are straight up and down, or we are on a slant; but no contortionist alive can be both leaning and walking upright at the same time!" The very thought of that discrepant proposition reminds me of a rather silly compendium of "good advice" that someone once compiled:

> Keep your shoulder to the wheel, your ear to the ground, and your nose to the grindstone; your eye peeled, your finger to the wind, and your back to the wall: march to the beat of your own drum, paddle your own canoe, and call your own tune. Meanwhile, hold your head up high, keep a stiff upper lip, and walk a straight furrow. And through it all, keep smiling—you're on Candid Camera!

Well, if you can accomplish all of that, you are indeed a most remarkable person! And the strange idea of leaning in order to walk uprightly may seem no less inconsistent and impossible than that inapt and incongruous set of mixed-up directions. But such is not the case.

Consider, for example, the literal meaning, and then the metaphorical and spiritual meaning, of the word "upright." Literally, to be "upright" means to be "on a truly vertical plane." One pictures something that is upright as being squarely perpendicular, as being simply straight up and down—in short, as being precisely what the Leaning Tower of Pisa is not. Last spring, we replaced an old plum tree that had stood in our back yard since well before we moved into our home. I had to cut that tree down because it had become so old and decrepit that it was in danger of falling down. But we did not leave the space where that tree had stood simply blank. Instead, we obtained, and planted in that part of our yard, a new, young and healthy plum tree that we hope will grow up to provide both fruit and shade for us in the coming years. And when I set that tree into the ground, I did a usual thing to go along with it. I drove a strong stake into the ground about a foot from the trunk of the sapling—(there's no buried telephone wire there!)—and tied the young tree to the stake in such a way that the trunk was as nearly perfectly vertical as I could make it. That was simply so that, as the tree grows, it will be upright. I don't want it growing at an angle. I want it to stand strong and straight over the entire course of its life. And that's an illustration of the literal meaning of the notion of uprightness—something you can check out with a plumb line.

But there is also a metaphorical and spiritual meaning to that term, as well; and this is the meaning that obtains in the usage of that word as we find it in the Bible. There, human beings are described as being optimally upright. And that does not refer to posture or physical bearing. It refers to integrity and moral rectitude—the condition of being a worthy, honest, and virtuous individual, numbered among those who, to employ yet another biblical metaphor, have "clean hands and a pure heart" (Psalm 24:4).

That sort of uprightness is the highest kind of achievement to which any person on the road to becoming might aspire. And that kind of uprightness—a virtuous expression of what it means to function as a human being made in the image of God and reflecting that image in and through one's person and deeds—is, as is the uprightness I hope for in my little plum tree, made assuredly possible by the process of deriving one's personal and spiritual alignment from a guiding and sustaining source. In the plum tree's case, it is the stake to which it is attached by means of a physical yoking. In your case and mine, it is the power and the purity and the presence of God Himself to which we relate ourselves through our reliance, our *leaning,* upon Christ the Lord. And this is not a static, fixed, or mechanical thing of which I speak—as though we might get ourselves tied to Christ in something of the same way in which Ulysses was lashed to the mast, so that we are no longer the architects and directors of our own destiny, and cannot even will our own way. "Leaning on Jesus, leaning on Jesus," as the old Gospel song tells of it, is not giving oneself over to some stultifying, frustrating and restricting process by which we are "cribbed, cabin'd and confined." Rather, it is opening ourselves up to the life-giving guidance and nourishment of that Spirit by which we are joined to Him. Our lives are still our own to lead, in the fullest sense of the word, just as the growth of my little plum tree is entirely dependent upon the maturational factors inherent in the tree itself. The stake upon which it "leans," so to speak, in order to direct it into uprightness, does not infringe in any way upon its own teleological drive to become the fullest example and expression of plum-tree-hood it can be. The stake only serves as a principle which makes that full development possible. And the gracious and guiding and empowering presence of Jesus Christ, likewise, does not in any way limit me in my quest for full personhood or take away from me the necessity for me to find and define my own soul as the *I* that I long to, and seek to, become. Rather, His supporting presence actually provides the design and the dynamism that make my true uprightness possible. And furthermore, whereas the plum tree is bound to its guiding stake only by an inert length of padded rope which transmits no vitality, I am wonderfully and potently united to Christ by the quickening linkage of His living Spirit.

If I am ever going to attain even a modicum of true and worthy uprightness, it is patently obvious to me that I will need something beyond myself to provide the motive and the power to accomplish that. And God has provided such a helping and upholding measure through the simple process of leaning. I find the strong and reassuring reality of His sustaining nearness to be a source of strength and confidence; and I find the life and love that He radiates from His person to mine to be an uplifting and purifying and enabling force for my own journey towards wholeness and fullness. "Forgive me if too close I lean/My human heart on Thee," wrote Whittier in one place.[1] Understandably so! For I must and will thus lean, because this is my only hope of ever being upright!

Leaning Strengthens Us To Fight The Good Fight

Each of us is aware that every new day brings with it a new challenge to live effectively and worthily as someone who is truly in the process of *becoming*. And what we need in order to face and meet that challenge is a spiritual resource that can empower us and direct us in a way that will make our journey towards full personhood a truly open and growing possibility and actuality.

The process of *leaning* is just the something that we can discover in this regard. Even when, as I once heard one commentator observe, we sometimes feel like a Maytag repairman who gets up one morning only to find that every washing machine in the world is broken, yet we can address the stresses and difficulties and hazards and risks and struggles of life with hope and assurance. We have Someone to lean on who will never intrude upon us or infringe upon the autonomy of our own personhood, but who is always there to support, encourage, sustain and enable us in our daily engagement of life. David, the psalmist, expressed this in some other very graphic and dynamic terms: "For by Thee have I run through a troop; and by my God have I leaped over a wall" (Psalm 18:29 KJV).

Whatever "walls" of circumstance or thought are standing between us and our full participation in the process of *becoming* will surely frustrate us and turn us away in bitterness and disappointment, unless we have the dynamic impetus of God's power to enable us to vault over them and continue on our way. Whatever "troops" of problems stand menacingly between us and the realization of our goal will frighten and deter us by their fierceness, unless we possess the courage and the might to sweep through them by the grace of God.

Truly, we never stand so freely and independently, we never assert the deep freedom and autonomy of our own person, we never choose our own way and discover our own future, nearly so much in any other way as when we *lean* in glad acknowledgement and fellowship on our strengthening and sustaining Lord.

Notes

1 John Greenleaf Whittier, 1807-1892, "I Bow My Forehead to the Dust," in *The Tent on the Beach and Other Poems,* 1867.

Chapter 13
All You Have To Do Is Be

MELODIOUS

I do not mean, when I indicate that we all should aspire to be melodious, that we all should also aspire to be practicing instrumentalists or vocalists. Rather, the quality to which I refer now has to do with what it is like when my deepest inner self harmoniously exults in a participation in what I sense to be the most profound and fulfilling realities of human experience—when I sense expansively that I am really "in tune" with all of life's dimensions and facets.

Being Melodious Means Being Tuned In To GOD

Think for a moment of the quality of perfectness with which creation was endowed in the beginning. Our world and everything in it was originally called into being with a sense of "just-rightness" about it. It was marked with the characteristics of being pleasant, fair, lovely, sweet, uplifting and excellent. Every part agreed with every other part. The cycle and flow of nature were perfectly balanced. There was nothing lacking, and nothing that was present was in any way jarring or upsetting. All was in perfect harmony; so much so that it is declared in marvelously symbolic terms, that, when the foundations of the earth were laid and the cornerstone thereof was set, "the morning stars sang together, and all the angels shouted for joy" (Job 38:7).

But as we know, that pristine harmony was about to be shattered. It was about to be marred by the discord and clangor of human sinfulness. Humankind threw the great created symphony off-key and out of tune, introducing the harsh notes of perversity and *hubris*. What had been a great sweeping melody of perfection now became a jangling dissonance of brokenness and incompleteness. And, if it is not too irreverent an image, one might almost picture God in this regard as clapping His hands over His ears and turning away from the cacophonic cat's concert that the world of human existence had become. Except, of course, that God did not turn away. The strident and discordant sounds that a bungled symphony of beauty became did not cause God to give up on our foolish and fumbling humanity. Instead, our need only moved Him to further action by which the lost grace and beauty of the world might be rediscovered and reclaimed; so that, again, if it is not too irreverent, one might imagine still another picture of God: this one with God—out of His concern and compassion towards His inharmonious creation—seeking longingly to bring that creation back to a healed and restored fellowship with Himself, by standing in grace before that creation almost like a divine Lawrence Welk, and, with baton poised at the ready, admonishing the world with inviting love and encouragement: *"An' a-one an' a-two!"* Well, that is, of course, highly symbolic; but it is not only symbolic. It is down to earth and practical, as well. Harmony and melody are terms that are marvelously suggestive in their meanings for us in our day-to-day life. They tell us that God is a God of beauty, order, loveliness, and grandeur. They impact upon our spirits with the impression that, in order to be in fellowship with this God, our own spirits and our own daily lives need to be lifted and purified and harmonized to the place where we do not represent discord and dissonance, but can take our place as worthy members of a universal chorus of praise and adoration and service.

Being Melodious Means Being Tuned In To LIFE

The outcome of our having become tuned in to God is summed up in terms of a further melody: "He put a new song in my mouth"(Psalm 40:3). And that makes a great difference in the way in which we respond to and deal with whatever comes into our lives.

It seems appropriate, for instance, to sing inwardly—and outwardly, for that matter, even if our talents are small, though the sweetest music will always arise from the heart and not the larynx—whenever anything happy or fortunate occurs. Which thought the writer of Psalm twenty-eight expressed very beautifully when he wrote: "The Lord is my Strength and my Shield; my heart hath trusted in Him and I am helped; therefore my heart danceth for joy, and in my song will I praise Him" (Psalm 28:8 BCP).

A dancing heart, a praising tongue and a bubbling spirit all just seem to go together. There are times when one simply has to sing, hum, whistle, yodel, dance, hop, skip or *something*, in order to give expression to the rejoicing and celebration that one feels on the inside. To squelch that inclination at such a time can only lead to dampening down the fires of life itself and smothering the very impulses of one's being—coming dangerously close, I must think, to just that kind of inappropriate response to God's promptings to life that St.

Paul warned about when he counseled, "Do not put out the Spirit's fire" (1 Thessalonians 5:19).

I recall something that a visiting minister shared once in a sermon preached at a Bible Conference, as this reflects on this matter. He told of his experience in connection with a young man whom he had baptized and received into church membership. It seems that this particular individual, at the time when the minister first met him, had been unaccustomed to any sort of church culture for all of his life. He was about eighteen years of age, but had had no exposure even to Sunday School. He knew nothing of what went on in a church and was quite unaware of how the Gospel might impinge on his life. But then, through an acquaintance with another young man who was a member of the pastor's congregation, he began attending services and paying heed to the message of the Gospel, which came as music to his ears. He felt challenged and invited by the presentation of the Gospel that he heard, and eventually came to confess his faith in Jesus Christ as his Lord and Savior, and thus came to be a candidate for baptism, which, according to the practice of the church, was believer's baptism by immersion. After receiving instruction and after having given testimony to the validity of his profession, the young man was scheduled to be baptized in a Sunday service. The evening of the baptism came around, and a large congregation gathered for what was anticipated to be a reverent and meaningful expression of worship. It was just that—but with a little bit of a twist that made it even more reverent and memorable than usual.

The service proceeded in a joyous but dignified manner, with several hymns, prayers, Scripture Lessons, and an appropriately topical sermon. And then came the time for the actual baptism, as the climax of the entire evening. The pulpit at the front of the sanctuary was adroitly moved aside to provide an unimpeded view of the baptistery to all in attendance; the curtains closing off the baptistery were dramatically pulled back, and there the pastor appeared standing hip-deep in the water, ready to receive the eager young candidate. The young man, obviously struck by the beauty and solemnity of the occasion, his face aglow with joy, made his way down the steps at the end of the tank and moved over to stand beside the pastor, who then addressed him in appropriately grave tones and led him in a confession of his faith as a witness to his readiness to enter into the highly symbolic act of baptism. Then, without further ado, the minister intoned the New Testament formula of Trinitarian authority, grasped the young man firmly by his shoulders, plunged him under the water, and then helped him to his feet as he resurfaced spluttering and gasping and wiping the water off his face. The newly baptized believer then regained his composure and stood, his long hair hanging in ringlets and a beatific smile upon his countenance, obviously rejoicing inwardly at the wonderful realization of what had transpired; and at that moment the minister raised his arm and stretched out his hand to pronounce a prayer of benediction over the head of the dripping neophyte. And that's when things took a little different turn.

To this point, the entire proceedings had progressed in a standard churchly way. The mood had been joyful and celebratory, yet suitably restrained and even sedate. But for the young man who was at the center of the evening, this last act of the minister's could mean only one thing, and that one thing was something dynamic and participatory. In his world, to lift the arm and extend the hand towards another person signified a move to express a jubilant "high five." Accordingly, as the minister appeared to be proffering this signal, the young man gleefully shot out his own right arm, loudly smacked his palm against the minister's, and shouted out with triumphant joy the single word of exultant exclamation, *"YES!"* That was something that the congregation was not prepared for! It was breaking new and unusual ground! But to the congregation's credit, instead of shrinking back from the high joy of that moment and retreating into pious propriety, they caught the melodiousness of the occasion, and the whole atmosphere of the service was suddenly freed up to become one of holy jubilation and thanksgiving. I think it would be safe to say that they went away from that service that night with their hearts *singing!*

I don't know how often we might have occasion to be a part of such a particular expression as that; but I do know that life does offer us many, many occasions when our hearts feel like dancing for joy and our tongues want to sing out our rejoicing. And our very souls and beings will be enriched and enhanced by our following through on that—maybe expressively, for everyone to see and hear; or maybe simply within ourselves, where the inner chorus of singing and exulting rises in our minds and spirits. I remember from my childhood days an old proverb that was common in the circles I knew. It was a real wet blanket, to be sure—a real "downer," as we would say now. It was the dire warning that predicted: "Sing before breakfast, cry before supper." What a cheerless philosophy! What a sad outlook indeed, if we are afraid to let the music within us out, lest some retributive kind of fate should lay on us a counterbalancing sorrow as a penalty for our impertinence! I say, "Let the music sound—before breakfast, after supper, and/or at any time prior to, later than, or in between!" I much prefer Jimmy Durante's old theme song that began, "You gotta start off each day with a song!" And I certainly like the sentiment of the old Spiritual that affirms simply, "I'm gonna sing when the Spirit says sing!" And one time when the Spirit says sing is when we have a joy or a gratitude or a thanksgiving to express.

But being tuned in to life and being therefore melodious does not mean that we sing only at the happy times. It is just as meaningful for us to give melodious expression to our sentiments when life is anything but bright and happy—which notion Jimmy Durante's song also emphasizes as it goes on to say more fully, "You gotta start off each day with a song, even *when things go wrong!"*

Not all music is as bright and as cheery as the grand finale of a Broadway musical! Not all singing is exultant, not all playing is *allegro,* not even all dancing is jaunty and jovial. Sometimes music is more somber, playing is more *adagio,* and even dancing is more pensive and restrained. One sings, plays or dances in such instances not just to rise on flights of exuberance but to give expression to the deepest and strongest currents of feeling within one's soul. And yet even here the melodious expression of one's true self and one's honest experience is constructive and therapeutic.

One only has to turn to the Book of Psalms to discern there the meaning and significance of being melodious in even the most difficult and crushing of life's experiences. The Psalms are, it has been said, "The Song Book of Ancient Israel." The Psalms are written to be sung, and the stereotype that most of us have had, probably since childhood, is a picture of David strumming on his harp while he and others joined in a sort of community sing-song to God, running through all the selections in the Psalter. That may or may not be an exactly accurate perception!—but there is certainly at least some truth to it. People did sing the Psalms. And they sang them often—sometimes together, as hymns or community expressions of faith; sometimes alone, as personal recountings before God of what was happening in their lives. And it is that latter kind of singing that I think is most significant in connection with the particular point of singing "even when things go wrong."

There is a whole category of psalms within the Psalter that reflects the notion of what is simply called "lament." This includes a number of individual compositions scattered throughout the entire collection, embodying the elements of complaint, fear, worry, loneliness, disappointment, anger, discouragement, doubt and even despair. These are songs, but songs in the minor key. Some of them are dirges. Some of them make the music we today call "the blues" seem downright cheerful by comparison! Some of them sound like the singer is about ready to throw in the towel on life itself and give up on God Himself. But the secret for the ancient writers of such psalms lay in the singing—just as the secret for the modern reader of such psalms lies in personally entering into, and apprehending, and expressing the sentiments declared so that the reader actually becomes at least an inward singer and finds meaning and significance and incredible help through truly participating in the music. This is a secret we can learn concerning being melodious in our lives even when the circumstances and events of life are difficult and dismal—even when, to use a phrase from the writings of the prophet Isaiah, we find ourselves having to "walk through the fire"(Isaiah 43:2). To sing in such a setting as that is to lift the soul out of a downward spiral of sorrow and despair up into an orbit of embracing life and living it through to the ultimate discovery of peace, purpose and meaning.

There is a delightful reflection on that in an old bit of folklore concerning the burning of a log in a wood-burning fireplace, specifically as that log seems to alternately sing and whistle as it burns. Elementary physics would explain that as the noise made by moisture and sap found within the wood. But there is a more imaginative explanation than that, one that trumps mere science with beauty. Accordingly, it is said that, while the tree from which the log came was growing in the forest, birds of various kinds came and nested and rested in its leafy branches. While there, the birds sang and trilled their heartfelt songs, and the sweet music of those songs sank deep into the heart and nature of the tree. Then, when the tree was eventually felled, and ended up as a log in the fireplace, the fire in which it found itself served to release the enclosed music so that the log sang sweetly and soulfully.

It is not fanciful bird-songs but factual personal determination that enables us, even in the fires of adversity, to sing from our hearts all the notes of the song of life.

Being Melodious Means Being Tuned In To OUR DEEPEST SELVES

Because we resonate to the harmony of our deepest persons, we may hear a melody that others know nothing of.

> Once a fiddler played so sweetly that all who heard him began to dance, and whoever came near enough to hear joined in the dance. Then a deaf man, who knew nothing of music, happened along; and to him all that he saw seemed the action of madmen—senseless and in bad taste.[1]

There is one particular expression used in The Book of Psalms that I believe gives a basic indication of what it means to be truly melodious in life. Singing to give expression to moods is common enough in our society. But what we said earlier about my singing because there is something tucked away inside me that is like the bird-song hidden in a log points up the fact that something much more profound than moods and ways to express and deal with those moods must lie behind a melodiousness in life that is genuine and valid. And that something has to do with the real persons that you and I are in our very most real self of selves. And that's what the expression from the Psalms that I referred to speaks about.

"Deep calls to deep," it is affirmed (Psalm 42:7). That is more than poetry. It is more than imagery. It is fundamental reality. Because it is, indeed, from the deepest places of our own being that we relate to and resonate to the deepest things of life. The vibrations of our truest selves—the most profound notes of genuineness and utter honesty—are what quiver in tune with the truly elemental happenings that we encounter and participate in in life. That's what we need to be in touch with and expressive of. And that's how we end up being melodious—which is to say, embracing a full and candid realization of, and expressing an unaffected and undissembling response to, whatever it is that we are really feeling and going through. It has been said that every person's life is like a great musical score. Then let us play the symphony that is our life's story! Like an Aeolian harp that faithfully produces the music for which it was made as the wind blows through its strings, so we are called upon to set forth faithfully the music that is of our essence as the winds of circumstance, events, and daily occurrences sweep over our lives. The song is you. Let the music begin.

Notes

[1] Martin Buber, *Tales of the Hasidim: The Early Masters* (New York: Schocken Books Inc., 1975) p.53.

Chapter 14
All You Have To Do Is Be
NATURAL

God created man in His own image, in the image of God He created him. Male and female He created them (Genesis 1:27).

When God made us He did so, we believe, not randomly but deliberately; and not in a cookie-cutter fashion, but specifically and discretely. Eve was Eve and Adam was Adam, each graced with the individual qualities that marked him or her as a singular and distinct person. And it is just that initial, divinely-granted individuality that, following in the plan and intention of God, we are to strive to realize and fulfill for ourselves in our generation. To that end we seek the goal of becoming, by His grace, the unique persons He designed us to be. This means that I am to become me, and you are to become you, as individual and singular persons, distinctly called to be ourselves and not some other self, of whatever description. What we seek to discover and express in our living is nothing less than the gift and goal of our own *me-ness* and *I-ness,* the real person, the true self that is free from artifice or affectation of any kind. To that end we seek to express the essential truth of who we are not by pretending, bluffing, acting or imitating, but by being *natural.* Harking back to the comic strip character, Popeye the Sailor Man, we simply affirm, "I yam what I yam."

The Natural Person Is Inner-BASED

"To thine own self be true." Those words spoken by Polonius to his son Laertes, in Shakespeare's play, *Hamlet,* have often been quoted as an encouragement and a directive to live with integrity and honor. Though in their original context they are certainly less high-minded than is commonly assumed, their thrust is nevertheless appropriate to the quest for one's personal best. "Be true to your own deepest and most genuine self; live by the convictions of your own heart and soul; act and speak according to your own inner judgment; be who you really are; act *naturally.*"

That's a piece of advice that St. Paul passed on in his letter to the Romans. "Don't let the world around you squeeze you into its mould" (Romans 12:1, J.B. Phillips). If it's not the dictate of your own heart and soul; if your own inner voice is telling you that you ought to do or say or think something else: then don't simply cave in to outer pressures or demands; do the natural thing, the thing that will be an honest and worthy expression of who you really are and what you really believe and how you really want to be in the world. It's you, not anyone else, who must be expressed through your living. And your actions must bear the stamp of what you feel and how you want to act.

There is a beautiful statement found in the book of Revelation that I believe adds something to this thought. There, the Lord Himself is pictured as speaking to persons who are seeking to find the fullest measure of becoming in knowing Him and His promise of life. In one place, the Risen Christ makes this promise: "I will give . . . a white stone, with a new name written on it, known only to him who receives it" (Revelation 2:17). I think a great deal should be made out of the imagery used there.

When you and I find our lives touched by the living Lord of life Himself; when we respond to His leading and drawing of our spirits so that we embrace and allow ourselves to be embraced by the love and purposes of our Creator and Redeemer; something by way of a transformation occurs. Our blindness is changed to sight; our deafness becomes hearing; our deadness becomes life! And that is symbolically expressed in a number of ways. We walk a different path now. We are headed in a new direction. We are powered by a new dynamic. And, we are *given a new name!* As the chorus of an old Gospel song puts it simply but exultantly, "There's a new name written down in glory; and it's mine, O yes, it's mine!" That's what Revelation 2:17 declares.

"I will give you a new name that no one but you and I will know," our Lord says. "This secret name is a part of the bond between your heart and Mine. I have written it in stone, and passed that stone on to you. Now, wherever you go, whenever any choice or decision is asked of you, take out that stone and read again that name that is yours from Me, that only you and I know and understand; and respond to your situation in such a way that you will be able to sign that beautiful and personal name as an ownership of your action. Don't hastily affix that name to deeds that are a shallow reflection of someone else's purposes; don't carelessly scrawl that name to endorse ends that are really at variance with your own deepest intent. It is a clean and precious and intensely personal name that can only be used by you, and that must be used by you in the traffic and to-do of life. Don't deny that name by tracing another signature set out for you to copy; and don't debase that name by using it to endorse anything that is unworthy."

I remember going through a phase when I was about eight or nine years old, when I was deeply dissatisfied with my name. Not my family name—that was what gave me my sense of rootedness and belonging in the world. No, what distressed me greatly was my given name—Tom, or Tommy, or Thomas, as the case might be, depending on the gravity or formality of the occasion. Why had my parents had to hang *that* on me? Why couldn't they have called me what a close friend of mine was called, a name that I deemed far superior to my own, a name that I would have been delighted to bear?—Why couldn't they have called me "Gerald"? Oh! I was galled by life's unfairness!—and even more so by the crushingly ironic fact that my parents had, in fact, given me that envied name of Gerald as my *middle* name, thereby depriving me forever of its beauty by tucking it away into obscurity and dooming it forever to the status of a middle initial. Couldn't I just ditch my given name and use my middle name? Couldn't I be allowed the inestimable joy of no longer being Tom, and of being, instead, Gerald? But, alas, no; Tom I was, Tom I had to be, and Tom I still am—(a reality which, incidentally, I now gladly and positively affirm).

I realize that not everyone has had the same kind of experience. In fact, there may well be persons reading these words for whom the notion of a name change has become not a lessening desire but a growing conviction and an ultimate decision. I remember reading in a magazine several years ago about a gentleman who lived, as I recall, in Decatur, Georgia, who went through the process of having his name legally changed from what he had been dubbed at birth to something more nearly reflective of how he saw himself. His original given name was Gary Eugene Duda. He went through the necessary court proceedings and had that changed to *Zippity* Duda. Apparently his friends had hung that nickname on him, and he had liked it and decided that it was him; so he became Mr. Zippity Duda. And I have always thought that it would be a delight to meet that person. Somebody who puts the word "Zippity" into his name sounds like what we would call "a fun guy;" and I have always pictured him as a truly upbeat sort of individual, who would express and conduct himself in accordance with the real person he realized himself to be.

The name by which I identify myself, and my embracing of that name in life, is of critical importance. I may readily accept and approve the name that my parents chose for me; or I may decide that I have to change it to reflect something that is more nearly who I am. But in any event, when I use or sign that name it is my *self* that I am identifying with whatever it is that I am endorsing. And that is something that I must never lose sight of on the more profound level of our identity before God. "You are *you!"* speaks the living Lord to each one of us, in affirmation of a personal, precious identity that is God-given in the most emphatic and powerful sense of that term.

Don't let anyone take that identity from you or persuade you to debase it, or entice you to forsake it. Live up to that secret and sacred name. You will live up to it worthily, if in all that you do or say you are truly inner-based.

The Natural Person Is Inner-DIRECTED

It occurs to me at this point that there might be some confusion in the minds of some of my readers with regard to my choice of terminology when I say that we must strive to be *natural.* Perhaps I should quickly double back here and set forth a necessary clarification. The confusion to which I allude may arise from the way in which the word "natural" is used in the New Testament, where, especially in the writings of St. Paul, to be *naturally* inclined is a negative idea, related to acting in a way uninformed or uninfluenced by the grace and power of God. "Natural" in this sense means "according to the base and even corrupt instincts of our nature," as opposed to "spiritual," which means "as influenced and directed by God." I do not use the term "natural" in this negative way. Rather, presupposing our openness to God and His influence in all our being and doing, I simply take "natural" to mean what is not affected or put on for any reason; what is the truest instinct of the heart, guided by the goal of my own deepest and most assured well-being and self-fulfillment. The inner-directed person knows that only thus can integrity and self-esteem be found; which calls to mind the following.

I remember hearing once about an imaginary interaction between those legendary literary characters, Dick and Jane, and their illustrious dog, Spot. (This didn't come from the pages of an elementary school reader, by the way!) It went something like this.

"Lie down, Spot, and play dead," says Jane. Spot continues to stand stolidly, making no move to comply.

"Stand up, Spot, and beg," says Dick. Spot doesn't even move a muscle.

The session goes on.

"Go fetch, Spot," Dick says, giving the ball a toss. No action from Spot.

"Roll over in the grass, Spot," says Jane. Spot doesn't even twitch.

So the encounter concludes, and is summed up this way: Dick and Jane think that Spot is a stupid, lazy dog. Spot, on the other hand, thinks that Dick and Jane are a couple of turkeys!

The inner-directed person can empathize with Spot. Who wants to go through life lying down or rolling over or playing dead at someone else's whimsical command? Or who wants to chase some meaningless ball just because somebody else thinks you should? "Atta boy, Spot!" one is inclined to say. "Don't just be putty in the hands of others! Follow the honest persuasion of your own heart. Let your actions be *natural,* in the sincere acting out of who you really are."

And again, a word of clarification is in order, to complement what has just been asserted, lest an overemphasis on being inner-directed should skew us out of balance in the total expression of our *being* and *becoming.*

I am not suggesting or proposing that any one of us should determine to be such a power-house of inner-directedness that we brush aside all expectations regarding our behavior, or throw off all constraints upon our self-determination, in order to "be our own person." To be inner-directed does not mean to be boorish, or irresponsible, or just plain "bull-headed." Rather, it just means that all of what we say and do is genuinely in keeping with the reality of our personhood. We know how to say "No," if the occasion demands it from us; and we know how to say "Yes," even if it might be more convenient or politically correct to say otherwise. But our "No" and our "Yes" are not merely crustily contrary on the one hand, or spinelessly acquiescent on the other. They are the honest expression of our truest selves, and as such they are set forth in a spirit of conviction and constructiveness. We must say "Yes" or "No," as the case may be, because that is what is required of us as we strive to live naturally.

The Natural Person Is Inner-RELATED

What I mean when I speak of being "inner-related" is actually something like what we mean when we use a term like "an integrated personality," or what we mean when we speak of someone who is really a "together" sort of person. Such an individual will be, as we have seen, inner-based and inner-directed because he or she is inwardly coherent—inwardly whole, inwardly right, and thus inwardly powered—with a balance and a configuration of one's true personhood that enables one to pursue, with all of one's heart and soul and mind and strength, the glorious goal of becoming one's best and fullest self.

Harry Emerson Fosdick once used a figure of speech that I think is highly illuminating in this regard. Some individuals, he said, are like a brush heap—a helter-skelter, miscellaneous jumble of twigs, branches and leaves; while some other persons are like a living tree—made up of, and employing, the same materials, but with a vastly different outcome. The brush heap has no unifying, vivifying center. And it will never grow—it will only become ever less and less of what it is. But a living tree is different. A tree has a center of aliveness, found in its roots, sap, and growing branches. It will blossom, and continue to grow, bearing appropriate fruit as the case may be, witnessing to the living entity that it is. "The basic urge of the human organism," Fosdick notes, "is toward wholeness. The primary command of our being is, 'Get yourself together;' and the fundamental sin is to be chaotic and unfocused."[1] The natural person is one who has made such a discovery and who has come, in that light, to the place where wholeness marks his or her person at the center, so that he or she lives fully and freely and wholeheartedly as a result.

Saint Paul, writing almost two thousand years ago, knew the secret of inner relatedness. And, what's more, he knew the secret of how any struggling, disoriented, fragmented individual might come to possess that desirable quality. He knew the way for a person who metaphorically was nothing more than a jumbled, lifeless brush heap to become someone aptly described as a tree, planted by the rivers of water, who brings forth fruit in the appropriate season, whose leaves do not wither, who flourishes and who abounds in deep and vital life (See Psalm 1). For St. Paul, and for countless persons since, the secret to vital, inner-directed personhood was simple, yet profound. It was and is, as we have noted before, "Christ in you, the hope of glory" (Colossians 1:27). When that tremendous factor becomes a reality in anyone's life—when Jesus the Lord becomes the guiding force within one's very life and being—to act naturally out of that glorious relationship will mean to act in the most constructive and fulfilling way possible. Thomas Merton puts this in a way that has radically opened up my own thinking in this regard, and that I hope will be of enlightenment to you. Following on the sincere declaration, ". . . Let Christ form Himself in you," Merton goes on:

> For as Christ unites in His one Person the two natures of God and of man; so too, in making us His friends, He dwells in us, uniting us intimately to Himself. Dwelling in us, He becomes, as it were, our superior self; for He has united and identified our inmost self with Himself. . . . A supernatural union of our souls with His indwelling Divine Person gives us a participation in His divine sonship and nature. A 'new being' is brought into existence. I become a 'new man;' and this new man—spiritually and mystically one identity—is at once Christ and myself.[2]

This is, I think, a daring and sweeping affirmation to make; and perhaps only a mystic of the stature of Thomas Merton would have the presumption to set forth such a declaration—speaking, as he does, of a "spiritual union of my being with Christ in one new person." But, logically, one wonders what else is to be made of such biblical evidences as St. Paul's frequent comments about our being made "partakers" of God's grace through the Gospel, as well as the plain statement by the writer of The Book of Hebrews that "we are made partakers of Christ' (Hebrews 3:14 KJV); or the word from 2 Peter 1:4, that there are given unto us "very great promises and precious, so that through them you may participate in the divine nature."

That's just what it means to live from one's center when Jesus the Lord is Himself the glory and the power of that center. Then it only becomes natural, in the best sense of the word, to take St. Paul's exhortation, "I urge you to live a life worthy of the calling you have received" (Ephesians 4:1), as the governing principle of one's life.

Notes

[1] Harry Emerson Fosdick, *On Being a Real Person* (New York: Harper and Brothers, Publishers, 1943) p. 28.

[2] Thomas Merton, *New Seeds of Contemplation* (New York: New Directions Publishing Corporation, 1972) p. 158.

Chapter 15
All You Have To Do Is Be
OPEN

An old Persian tale tells of an illiterate beggar who somehow came into the possession of a beautiful ruby that was obviously very precious and valuable. He offered it for sale to a very wealthy merchant, expecting to realize a huge amount of money for something so rare and exquisite. In fact, he boldly asked for a price of one hundred rupees. He was most pleasantly surprised when the merchant simply met his price and purchased the gem without quibbling. After the transaction was completed, the merchant asked the man why he had asked so little for such a valuable commodity. "I would have paid you much more than one hundred rupees," he said. The poor illiterate beggar was dumfounded. "I did not even know that there was any price higher than one hundred rupees!" he said.

"There are more things in heaven and earth, Horatio, than are dreamed of in your philosophy."[1] Thus spoke a pensive Hamlet to his friend, enunciating a truth that applies right across the board in life. Too often, like Horatio, and like the beggar mentioned in the story above, we are blind to the many possibilities and nuances of living by which we are virtually surrounded. Too often, instead of being tuned in to the rich varieties of stimuli that could impinge on our thinking and our awareness to make us more cognizant of and engaged with all the rich layers of life, we are ignorant of and *closed to* that which lies beyond our established "philosophy." Impulses and opportunities that could push back the horizons of our lives and enrich us through personal expansion and growth go unnoticed or unappropriated. Oh! That we might be more *open* to everything that there is for us as the gifts of God in a life that is broad and rich and fulfilling!

Being Open Asserts That All Of Life IS A PROCESS

Consider the following personal observation. A few years ago, my wife and daughter and I had the privilege of spending a month's holidays in Great Britain. We toured fairly extensively and saw a great deal of the beauty of that nation; and there is a great deal of beauty to see. Among the lovely spots and areas that attract and impress visitors, the most beautiful and appealing of all, for me, at least, are the Yorkshire Dales. And thereby hangs a tale.

We were out driving one day in one part of the Dales when we came upon a natural phenomenon that drew our attention and led us to stop and gaze for a while. There was a deep fissured opening in the ground that tourists found worth looking at, and, indeed, a number of sight-seers' cars and even a couple of tour buses were parked around this particular spot. We were impressed by the sheer beauty of that natural formation; but there was something else that drew my attention even more forcefully. I had wandered away just a little bit from where so many others were, when I lifted up my eyes to gaze on the scene before me and around me; and at that point I stood literally transfixed. What I saw was without a doubt the most beautiful scene I had ever gazed on. Talk about the beauty of God's handiwork! I stood there with a feeling that I can only describe as one of reverence and awe as I looked out over the panorama before me. There was a high hill, with a stone fence snaking up one side of it; sheep were grazing on the hillside, the white of their coats contrasting sharply against the deep green of the grass; there was a stream in the valley below, with wild flowers lining it and verdant trees growing alongside it; and the whole sight was bathed in the soft and glorious light of the sun which was shining through the billowy white clouds that decorated the beautiful blue sky. I was so awe-struck by all of that that I simply stood still and let my soul drink it all in, allowing the beauty to engulf me. And then I knew what I must do. I must take a picture of all of this, so that I would have it always to treasure and to wonder at. So I took the picture—a color slide—standing back to get the widest camera angle possible, making sure that I got everything in.

After we got back home and had the pictures of our trip developed, we set up the projector and the screen one evening and set out to re-live the moments and days that we had so much enjoyed. I especially looked forward to my picture of the idyllic scene that had so enraptured me at the time—truly, the high spot of my experience, something to virtually bask in as I looked back at it. And finally, as our rehearsal of our holidays progressed, we came to the picture of my treasured spot in the Dales. The slide was flashed onto the screen, and there before my eyes stood that scene that had so impressed and delighted me. But, do you know what I saw, there in the family room of my own home? Well, I did not see once again—or at least I did not *feel* and *enter into* once again—the same glorious scene that had originally so enraptured me. What I saw was a picture of some sheep grazing on a hillside, a stone fence thereon, with some trees and flowers and a stream below, over-arched by a cloud-studded sky. It was all nice enough; but I could not recapture the depth and the intensity of what that scene had originally meant to me. And from that experience, I learned a lesson that applies right across the board in life; which is, that you simply cannot stop the ongoing stream of life at any one spot, because life does, indeed, go on; and the only way that you can avoid being left behind is to "go with the flow." You cannot capture and hold or freeze the past, no matter how delightful or beautiful it might have been, no matter how dear or precious you might have found it. Oh, to be sure, we can and ought to be *enriched* by the past, and we can be *nurtured* by the past even in the act of remembering it; but we cannot *depend on* the past for the needs of the present or the hopes of the future. I still get pleasure out of that slide whenever I show it; but I also understand that it is not a fond recollection of that scene and its moment of splendor, but my openness to the ongoing events of life that will allow me to continue to grow as a person. And maybe there's another setting—and maybe many more than one—totally different from the setting in Yorkshire but equally as awe-inspiring, awaiting discovery by me as I journey towards wholeness and fullness of person. And maybe that new scene is actually to be found within the very common and humdrum circumstances of my daily life. (God does not work only during sight-seeing vacations in a far away country!) So I am led to embrace and appreciate *all* of life as it comes. There is beauty and meaning just waiting for me to find. I don't want to miss any of it by failing to be *open* to what life is sending me moment by moment!

And that makes me think of something else that I want to share along this line—a particular verse of Scripture; one that just happened, as they say, to "grab" me in a meaningful way as I read it. This comes from the twelfth chapter of Acts, where the story is told of Peter's miraculous escape from prison through the ministry of an angel. In the part of the story where the angel awakens Peter and tells him to get his clothes on because he's getting out of prison, the wording in the New Revised Standard Version is a little different from the wording that I have read in other translations; and that's what caught my eye. I quote:

> Suddenly an angel of the Lord appeared, and a light shone in the cell. He tapped Peter on the side and woke him, saying "Get up quickly." And the chains fell off his wrists. And the angel said to him, "Fasten your belt, and put on your sandals, and follow me." Acts 12:7-8 NRSV.

When I first read those words—"Fasten your belt,"—what popped immediately into my mind through the process of association was the common expression that is used to warn somebody, in an airplane or a car, about the imminence of increased acceleration or some form of uncertainty or turbulence in the journey ahead: "Fasten your *seat-belt!"* And I was thrilled to think that that was just about what the angel was really saying to Peter: "Peter, fasten your seat-belt! Get ready for a surge of forward action! The dismally static situation you are in is about to become a dramatically dynamic one through a process of change!" And I like to think that that whole story from the Bible could be seen as a paradigm for each one of us as God addresses us through whatever circumstances He sends our way: "Fasten your seatbelt! There's challenging action ahead!" And we need to be *open* to the process that God constantly calls us to be a part of.

Being Open Asserts That Life IS OFTEN SURPRISING

We all have had the experience of being surprised by what happens in the course of our living. Life has a way of taking unexpected twists and turns, and even loops and flips! Factors that we never thought of come into play. Events that we could never have foreseen occur. And in and through all of that, life becomes more interesting, more graced with possibilities, and more potentially fulfilling.

Thus, consider in this regard a verse of Scripture that says something about what will hopefully be our basic stance toward life and all its vagaries. Writing in the Book of Hebrews, the author there sets out something that stands as a kind of litmus in the approach we take to the uncertain unfolding of our life story. "We," the writer says, boldly and declaratively, "are not among those who draw back from, or shrink from, life. Rather, we are among those who reach out to grasp life and live it to its fullest measure, allowing God to lead us—and, very frequently, to *surprise* us" (Hebrews 10:39 paraphrased.) Someone once called God "The Supreme Playwright." That's an insightful description. It speaks graphically of the way in which, time and time again, we seem to find "written in" to our life's surroundings new and creative factors that, much like elements in a play, give a whole new and profound twist to the way things then go on to occur. Which means we should never be bored, or overwhelmed, or defeated, or hopeless; because no matter how little meaning or joy or possibility we may see in our setting at any given moment, God is never at a loss to be able to "write in" something quite unforeseen and even wondrous into the script of our lives. His creativity is beyond our knowing or imagining; and we should never lose our attitude of hope and expectancy. We simply don't know where God is going to put a period in the story of our lives. Sometimes it's not a period at all, but just a comma or a semicolon of interlude; or maybe a question mark of possibility; or even an exclamation mark of amazement! Always, as long as there remains a breath in our bodies, we are faced with—at the very least—the open-endedness of the trailing dots . . . .—which reminds me of a simple but profound old saying that I have heard and that I heartily endorse: "With God, there is never a final straw!" We should never close off the possibilities of our lives until God, the great creative Playwright, has put His period of death at the end of our lines. Until then, as long as we're still in the drama of life, there's no telling how God will surprise us with new and fulfilling options and possibilities.

Being Open Asserts That Life IS REALLY ABOUT GROWTH And CHANGE

There is a very fancy word that philosophers and theologians use some times when they want to say something very profound and yet very simple about who we are and where we are going. The word is "teleology." It comes from a Greek word which speaks of the notion of the fulfillment of a designed purpose. Used in connection with human life, it refers to the belief that there is a purposive goal towards which all life is created by God to proceed; all of which can be put in very clear and ordinary language. Just as teleology, for instance, affirms that there is something built into an acorn so that that acorn is irresistibly drawn to become a towering oak tree; so teleology posits an innate and essential drive or compulsion within our makeup which draws us on to truly become that which God, our Creator and Designer, has intended us to be. Acorns don't end up as elm trees, or as rose bushes, or as ragweed. Their teleological destiny does not allow for that. An acorn unfolds in its life process to become one thing and one thing only—a grand and glorious oak tree. Even so, teleology says that we, as human beings made in the image and likeness of God and endowed by our gracious Creator with the destiny to express to the fullest measure possible His glorious design for us, are not intended to become stunted or twisted or blighted scrubs of persons. Oh, it's possible for us to end up that way—all too possible, unfortunately—and too many persons seem almost satisfied if that's all that they ever develop into. But that's not the way it's supposed to be! Our divinely-intended destiny belies that sad and inferior outcome. Rather, we are meant by our God to grow into vigorous and vital persons as we go through life in His favor and by His grace, following, and being drawn on by, and even being compelled by, those awarenesses and opportunities that lead us out into the beckoning future. We need to be open to all the influences that surround us and stretch out before us and impinge upon us. These are very often the very things that, as we confront them and work through them, are meant by God to strengthen us and equip us for our teleological unfolding and becoming.

Recall the story that Jesus told, which we call "The Parable of the Talents," but which should more properly be termed "The Parable of the Three

Servants"(Matthew 25:14-30). The master in that story went away for an indefinite time, leaving each of the three servants some money to handle during his absence. One man was given five "talents,"—a talent was the equivalent of about fifteen years' wages—another was given two talents, and the third man received one talent. The accounting for these deposits would take place, then, at the master's return. As it turned out, the master did not reappear for an extended period. In the meantime, the servants had to do something with the money that they had received, since they knew that the master would expect some sort of benefit from the funds that he had provided. The master finally returned and then called his servants to a reckoning. The servant who had received five talents was able to report to the master that he had earned five more, making a total of ten; and the man with two talents reported that he, also, had doubled his money into four talents. But the man who had received one talent had to acknowledge that he had not increased it at all. But, at least, he said, he hadn't lost any of it! There was the original deposit, unchanged, just as he had received it; and that's what he gave back to the master.

The parable is a parable of judgment—of judgment that the persons involved actually brought on themselves. The first two servants were commended and rewarded; the third was not affirmed and was, instead, reproved for his attitude of fearfulness and stagnation. And that's what the story is about. It's not about making smart investments in the stock market, or buying the right mutual funds, or even just socking your savings safely away in a guaranteed investment certificate. It's about what you do with your life. You may think that you have a lot of possibilities and options regarding what you can do with your interests, your commitments, and your involvements. You may be a five-talent person. Or you may see yourself as being limited in what might be open to you—a one-talent person, at best. That's not the point. The point is that, whatever you have or whoever you are, the essential you is challenged and called to grow towards further being and becoming. And the quality that will determine the degree to which we do or do not pursue the riches of personhood that are out there for us to discover and apprehend, is the quality of *openness.*

"Then will the eyes of the blind be *opened*" (Isaiah 35:5). May it please God that not only our eyes, but all of our physical and emotional and spiritual senses may be purposefully and courageously and determinedly open as we move through life on our journey towards becoming.

Notes

1 William Shakespeare, 1564-1616, *Hamlet,* Act 1, scene 5.

Chapter 16
All You Have To Do Is Be
PURPOSEFUL

"Dare to be a Daniel, dare to stand alone," an old Sunday School song says; "dare to have a purpose firm, dare to make it known." That's a very solid and necessary piece of advice; because without a *purpose* to hold us and guide us, without an explicit and explicable *raison d'etre*, we tend simply to drift in life, letting things happen as they will and simply trying to adjust to circumstances and roll with the punches as best we may. That's like a mariner sailing without any sense of a North Star by which to chart a meaningful and decisive journey. Serendipity—the practice of making happy discoveries and falling into pleasant turns of events by chance, as things just unfold before us—can be a pleasant reverie that we may entertain on occasion, but as a way of life it falls woefully short when it comes to living with meaning, vigor and fulfillment. We will never hit the bull's eye in life if we have no idea of what we are really aiming at. What we need is a compelling and overriding *purpose* in life to give focus, intention and direction to our existence.

To Live Purposefully Is To Live COMMITEDLY and REVERENTLY

"Submit to God, and be at peace with Him; in this way prosperity will come to you. Accept instruction from His mouth, and lay up His words in your heart"(Job 22:21-22). Commitment—the assured placing of utter confidence in and reliance on the Almighty in the face of everything, good or bad, that comes into our lives, and the glad responding to His counsel—is an attitude that rests on the wisdom and goodness of God in directing our lives. It is the conviction that is able to say:

> I know not what the future hath of marvel or surprise,
> Assured alone that life and death God's mercy underlies. [1]

Out of such a conviction one lives with a deep sense of settledness and sureness concerning the basic framework of life. A confidence in God that creates an attitude of trust, and issues in a response of commitment, is something on which we can rest assuredly. This is a confidence that says that, no matter what else may go right or wrong in life, we stand squarely on the sure rock of God's eternal sovereignty and power, with the firm purpose to be aligned with and expressive of that sovereignty and power. The Psalmist puts it beautifully:

> God is our refuge and strength, an ever-present help in trouble. Therefore we will not fear, though the earth give way and the mountains fall into the heart of the sea; though its waters roar and foam, and the mountains quake with their surging (Psalm 46:1-3).

The conditions pictured in Psalm 46 surely comprise what our modern jargon would define as a "worst-case scenario!" And actually, they remind me of something that I saw in a store window recently as I was walking along the street, window-shopping, in my home town. Set up in the window of a toy and novelty store on the main street was a display featuring three board games that I had never heard of or seen before. I'm quite used to the old standard games, such as "Monopoly," or "Risk," or "Clue," and the like; but these games were obviously nothing so tame. By their very names, and by the lurid illustrations on their box covers, they gave the impression of being extremely dramatic and exciting. They certainly caught my eye and piqued my interest! They were set up in what I'm sure the store's proprietor intended to appear as a progressive kind of intensity and significance; and that's the way they impressed me. Their names—garishly illustrated with appropriate graphics in each case—were: "Snowstorm!"—(You could almost feel the icy peril of being lost in a blizzard); "Earthquake!"—(Safety for the winner of the game, I guess, sheer terror for the loser); and "War!"—(With victory or annihilation seemingly the only options). And as I looked at those games, and sensed my progressively quickening pulse as I scanned them, ending up with the dreaded prospect of World War Three, I wondered "Wow! Where could you go from there?" Well, I came up with a possibility. How about one more game to end all games, this one to be called "Apocalypse!"? Which made me think further, with a confidence unshaken by the clever and effective window display, that even there—in, and through, and beyond snowstorm, earthquake, war, and/or even the ultimate concept of apocalypse—an attitude of trust in the person and purpose of Almighty God makes it possible to live and function confidently and meaningfully.

And our confidence will be logically and naturally coupled with *reverence* in our living, as well, as we seek to live purposefully. And reverence I would define simply not just as a forced or sullen acknowledgement of God as the Supreme Being who rules all things, and is over us because He is bigger and stronger than we are and can therefore do as He likes; but, rather, as a glad and loving recognition of the One whose eternal goodness and beauty are so profoundly revealed in His bestowal of Himself within our lives that we are led to bow in loving humility and confess His graciousness with hearts moved by awe and gratitude. Reverence is an attitude that recognizes God as being worthy of our worship and honor not just because of what He does or what we hope He might do, but because of who and what He is in His very person. Such a sense of reverence must characterize the one who would seek to live purposefully. Without our deep acknowledgement of Him, without our hearts and our minds being set to know Him and His will, we can never truly share His purpose as we seek to live with purpose ourselves. But when we live in a confidence that He is the center of our life, then our lives will have purpose and meaning as they share in His purpose and meaning.

To Live Purposefully Is Not To Act ARROGANTLY Or SELF-CENTEREDLY

Nobody wants to surrender his or her purpose in life, and no one should. But sometimes the determination to hold firmly to one's own purpose goes beyond a healthy self-confidence and self-assertiveness to an unhealthy resentment towards, and rejection of, any influence or input or ultimate welfare of others. It's one thing to "do it my way." That can have noble and effective results. It's quite something else to plunge ahead stubbornly and recklessly, intent on fulfilling my intentions, heedless of any respect for and consideration of other persons in my world. That can have ignoble and even calamitous effects—as a little story about a boy named Lester may illustrate.

A number of years ago, our family, comprised of my wife and me and our two children, lived in a small village where our home backed on to a large wooded tract through which ran a gentle, meandering stream. The woods were ideal for hiking and walking, and our children and their friends would often spend a summer day on a trek through the trees. The incident I want to tell you about took place on one such day when a group of seven or eight youngsters got together for such an excursion. It was early summer, a lovely mild day, and it was decided that each boy or girl would bring a packed lunch so that the gang could have a picnic at noon in the great outdoors. Accordingly, the various mothers involved had prepared for their offspring sandwiches of such usual fares as peanut butter and jelly, or scrambled eggs, or cold meat, along with cookies and fruit, with a large thermos of water provided by my wife for everyone to share. That took in all the children—everyone, that is, except Lester. When it came time to have their lunch, all present gathered around on a grassy spot and unwrapped the provisions they had brought—all, that is, except Lester. Oh, no! None of that humdrum, run-of-the-mill stuff for Lester! No, he had something special, something unique. He unpacked not sandwiches, but a hot dog and bun. And he would not be standing in line for a drink of water, either. He had gone one better than that, and had brought along a bottle of Pepsi-Cola.

With a flourish, he set about preparing his elegant repast. He opened his bottle of soda pop and set it down on a small ledge of rock, and then turned to prepare his main course. He quickly gathered several tufts of dried grass and some small dried twigs, arranged them as judiciously as any woodsman might, and then produced from his jacket pocket a small box of matches with which his mother had entrusted him for this occasion. He lit his cooking fire, and then proceeded to take a long stick with a pointed end, to which he affixed his hot dog, and began to roast the delicious looking morsel over the flames. That's when his downfall began. What Lester had not counted on was the fact that the stick he was using as a spit was just as flammable as the wood that was doing the cooking. He came to that realization shortly, however, when the stick caught fire and burned through, with the result that the hot dog dropped right into the heart of his makeshift grill! Thinking quickly, Lester whipped off his jacket and began to beat out the blaze in order to rescue his lunch. Unfortunately, he was somewhat careless in the way he handled his jacket, and was startled to see that the jacket had caught fire and was in danger of going up in flames. Thinking instinctively, Lester reached for the only liquid he had at hand, which was his Pepsi-Cola, and doused most of that drink onto the jacket to save it. The balance of the liquid he then poured onto the remains of the fire in the hope that he could rescue some edible vestige of his hot dog from the ashes. But alas! Lester's grandiose meal was not to be realized in any way. The charred relic of his hot dog was inedible, his Pepsi-Cola was completely expended, and, morosely, he had to console himself with just the kind offers of shared sandwiches from the other members of the group to go along with his dry and empty bun, followed by a drink of just plain water.

For most us, the results of whatever ill-advised or ill-considered actions we might be guilty of because of pride or one-upmanship will probably (and hopefully!) not be quite so dramatic or so deflating. But those results can be just as real. It is right, as we noted at the head of this chapter to have "a purpose firm." But that purpose must be a worthy expression of our deepest selves, and to that end needs to be properly focused not just on ourselves, not just on caring for, and looking out for, and taking care of "number one," but on God and His purpose for us in the world. That purpose is something that is appropriately expressed in community. "Each of you should look not only to your own interests, but also to the interests of others"(Philippians 2:4). "There is a way that seems right to many persons, but it turns out to be a dead end" (Proverbs 16:25, paraphrased). If my purpose is to know and to be aligned with the will of God as I respond to His claim on my life, then I may have the assurance that an appropriate outcome will come to me in the form of my knowing and living a life of meaning and effectiveness, and I will not end up in some dead-ended alley of meaninglessness and frustration. This does not necessarily mean that everything that happens in my life, then, will be good and productive in and of itself. Rather, it means that, with my eye on the purpose and goal of living my life as an expression of God's life in me and through me, everything that happens in my life will be amenable to my living it out in a way that leads me on to my goal of *becoming* the full person God has called me to be.

To Live Purposefully Means That We Are GRACEFULLY ASSERTIVE

I chose the words "gracefully assertive" because I believe they provide a perfect balance. A gracious and considerate person does not need to be a pushover, with a spine like mashed potatoes. He or she can and should, and indeed, must, live with vigor, forcefulness and determination. He or she must live out of the base of a strong purpose, which is essentially to honor God's purpose of becoming his or her truest and best self.

There is an illuminating insight into this reality portrayed for us in the New Testament in connection with an incident in the life of Jesus. In one setting, Jesus is challenged by those who thought that He should act and speak more in accordance with the agenda that they would set out. They didn't like His independence and His self-assurance. They didn't like the fact that He seemed to act out of an inner persuasion that could not be deflected or suppressed, and that He would not be answerable to them. They were, simply, blind to the fact that His life's purpose was so immersed in the purpose of God that He followed a course dictated by His utter identification with the will of God. So they confronted Him with a question that many a deliberately purposeful individual has heard at some time or another: "By what authority are you doing these things?" they asked. "And who gave you authority to do this?" (Mark 11:28). In other words, to put it in more modern terms, "Who do you think you are, anyway?" Jesus' answer was masterful. He did not strive to justify Himself to His questioners; nor did He cave in to them, and try to satisfy them. Instead, He simply foiled them through a question of His own that truly "hung them out to dry." He challenged them on their own non-recognition and non-acknowledgement of authority regarding their past experience with John the Baptist; and then, when his questioners' final response was to decline to answer Jesus' pointed query to them, His concluding assertion, as a summing-up of His own inner certitude and equilibrium, was the calm and self-assured declaration, "Neither will I tell you by what authority I am doing these things" (Mark 11:33), which is to say "I don't need to tell you by what sanction I am being Me in the expression of My personhood!" I find that expression of Jesus a most refreshing and encouraging one. It comes from the lips of the One who was the most courteous and compassionate individual who ever walked the earth; and yet it comes with an iron firmness that bespeaks a purposefulness that is unmistakable and profound.

To Live Purposefully Means To AIM NOBLY And HIGH

I ran across an example of expressed and accomplished purpose once, a number of years ago now, as I was reading, of all things, an obituary—the death notice of the prominent American businessman, Mr. Frederick Rand Weisman, whose passing was noted with international interest. In his lifetime, Mr. Weisman made a fortune in the automobile sales business, and he shared most generously out of that fortune, giving really quite magnificently to charities of various kinds and encouraging his fellow multi-millionaires to do likewise with their accumulated wealth. The recounting of his career was very impressive in its outlining of the various accomplishments of his life and the wide range of contributions and services that he had offered. But what really struck me in the whole account that I read about Mr. Weisman was something that was included almost as an aside in describing him. It was what was said to be his own favorite story about himself. And when I read that story, I thought I understood better the reason that Frederick Rand Weisman was the remarkable kind of man that he was.

It was really a very simple story. It concerned his own symbolic choice of a middle name. You see, Frederick Weisman was the son of Russian-Jewish immigrant parents who had come to the United States of America almost totally unlearned and with virtually no money or other resources. And what they had given their son—all that they had been able to give him—was minimal by any standards. His beginnings were truly humble beginnings; and the poverty of his circumstances was really sort of symbolized in the fact that he had been given only one first name—almost as if that was all his parents could afford!

Well, while Frederick Weisman was in university, on his determined way to becoming all he could become, he decided that he would adopt the cultural custom that he saw all around him and bestow upon himself a second name, a middle name. That was important to him as a part of his growth as a person.

So, walking out one day into the city of Minneapolis, where he was attending university, he looked up all around him at the skyline of that great city, and chose a name for himself based on what he saw there. His eyes rose to search over that skyline and his gaze came to rest on the tallest building of all, the one that—above all the others there—seemed to reach up, and soar towards the very heavens above. It happened to be the headquarters of the Rand Corporation, and it was known simply as "The Rand Building," identified by the single name emblazoned across its top: "RAND." In view of that, from that moment on, just plain Frederick Weisman became Frederick *Rand* Weisman. And his life went on to be marked by a height and even a grandeur of personal aspiration and awareness and achievement that impressively matched the choice that he had made.

One could not do better, we would say, than to be guided thus by one's highest aspirations. To deliberately make those lofty aims the ideal which actually names and identifies one's very self is an act of high commitment and purpose. "I delight to fulfill Thy will, O my God; Thy law is within my heart . . . ." I am utterly *purposed.*" (Psalm 40:10, Psalm 17:3 BCP).

Notes

[1] John Greenleaf Whittier, 1807-1892, from his poem, *The Eternal Goodness,* 1867.

Chapter 17
All You Have To Do Is Be
QUIET

"Where there's life there's noise," would seem to be a fair assessment of much of our world today. Whether it's incessant background music in elevators, offices, stores, restaurants and even hospital operating rooms; or just plain talk, talk, talk used to fill up all the empty spaces in our relating to one another, everywhere we go we seem to be confronted by, and even engulfed by, a virtual sea of sound. But there's a limit! There comes a time when noise should cease—a time when silence is called for, and when any individual who is seeking the fullness of person to which we are all called should simply learn to be quiet.

I Can't Even Hear Myself Think!

Silence can attest to and underline the importance of interiority in life. Being *quiet* allows us to discover the source of strength and meaning found within us. We are nourished and sustained in all our busyness and activity not by more and more data or louder and louder information, but by a deeper and deeper, strangely voiceless, realization. Consider in this regard a bit of insightful trivia.

Do you know what is the *second* most widely read book in the world?

You probably know what the *first* is. It is that perennial best seller, the most popular volume ever printed anytime, anywhere—the Bible. I'm sure that that doesn't surprise anyone. After all, that book has been seen for centuries as "the *good* book," wherein God and humanity meet, wherein humanity finds the explanation and the *raison d'etre* of its very existence; and it just makes sense that the most popular book of all time should be the one which is able to grasp and calm our rushed and fevered spirits and instruct us for living out our Creator's gracious intention for us. And if we can be quiet and attentive long enough, that's exactly what can happen.

But, to go back to our trivia question: if the Bible is the first most popular volume in our society, what is the second? And the answer is: *The Guinness Book of World Records*. And that fact, itself, speaks volumes!

To be sure, the Guinness Book is interesting, and it makes entertaining and even fascinating reading. Of course it's constantly being revised and updated, and although my own copy is getting somewhat dated now, I do appreciate and enjoy referring to it. But think of the contrast of ideas to be observed between the world's number one and the world's number two best sellers!

"Be *still,*" the Bible instructs us: "Be inwardly *quiet;* and learn thus the deepest meanings of God for your life" (Psalm 46:10, paraphrased).

Not so the Guinness Book! It takes off in the opposite direction. Here, this volume asserts, is the record of anyone and everyone who has run faster than anyone else has ever run, or jumped higher than anyone else has ever jumped; or who has thrown something that is heavier than, or lifted something that is bigger than, anything anyone else who ever lived has picked up or thrown; and/or who has run with, jumped over or in any other way exhibited a superlative degree of mastery with, to, on, or at anything you can think of, and some things you would never think of! Truly, this is a book whose principle rests on the notion of activity and accomplishment; and if you want to make the grade here, it has to be on the ground of outperforming, i.e., outrunning or outscoring or outwitting or outtalking or outlasting or in some other way just generally outshining all other comers. And one is impressed that there certainly are no cobwebs or flies or dust on anyone who has managed to make it to the pages of this singular book!

Well, I have no argument with *The Guinness Book of World Records* or with its concept. That book plays a fitting role in our society and it has earned its great popularity. I would only observe that, with regard to our quest for ultimate *being* and *becoming,* it also affords an opportunity for a meaningful reflection; something which may perhaps be best summed up and expressed in the words of an anonymous poem dating from the fifteenth century, that speaks for itself:

> Thou shalt know Him when He comes not by any din of drums,
> Nor the vantage of His airs, nor by anything He wears—
> Neither by His crown, nor His gown.
> For, His presence known shall be by the holy harmony
> That His coming makes in thee.[1]

That calls for the important qualities of inwardness and receptivity in order that we may begin to learn and know and grow. And, though it may sound like a contradiction in terms, it leads us to the essential understanding that, in our pursuit of personal wholeness, sometimes all we have to do is just be *quiet.*

Sometimes There Is A Quieting FROM

This is the basic kind of quietness that has been alluded to already. It is a silence into which we withdraw in order that outer distractions, interruptions, and claimant demands may be silenced. This is the kind of quiet to which we aspire when we are overburdened with, and even overwhelmed by, the grinding reality that Wordsworth stated so simply and yet so powerfully in his oft-quoted words, "the world is too much with us." This is the kind of quiet that we are seeking when we say, sometimes, that we would like to "get away from it all," when we are looking for "some space for ourselves," indeed, when all we really want is "a little peace and quiet." And usually we are led or driven to seek such a time of quiet because we find our emotional and spiritual receptors getting overloaded, and our minds feeling jaded. We find life becoming heavy and dull or flat and stale, and our inner resources riding close to empty; and we need somehow to get ourselves revitalized and renewed and regrouped in order to carry on meaningfully and effectively.

I remember something that spoke to me along this line, several years ago now, in connection with the Christmas season and Christmas shopping. I was browsing in a retail catalogue store one day in one December when I came upon a shelf full of articles that had been marked down and placed on sale because of some imperfection or flaw that each of them had. They were one-of-a-kind clearance items, each bearing a little note explaining why it was being sold for such a low price. There was, for instance, a jigsaw puzzle on sale, showing a beautiful picture on the front of the box but bearing the stark warning, "pieces missing." There was also a fluffy wind-up dog that could only stand, motionless and silent, and look at you because, as the accompanying notation tersely explained, "Spring broken." And so it went—an interesting but motley collection of imperfection. And then there was one other item there that really caught my eye, for two particular reasons.

One was that it was by far the largest and most elaborate article on the shelf. It was some kind of a marbles game, apparently supposed to be played within two large hemispheres of clear plastic with a number of slots and alleys and numbered pockets along the inner walls of the impressive dome that the two hemispheres formed. Inside, at one end, was a shooting device intended to propel marbles of various hues out into the works, and, obviously, into the numbered openings. It looked both challenging and inviting, and I could see why anyone would be drawn to engaging with it to see how great a score one could rack up. It was large, elaborate and imposing. But the little note attached to it to indicate its shortcoming was what really got my attention. It said simply and precisely: "Coming Unglued!" I almost felt impelled to take that explanatory note, stick it on my own forehead, and honestly say, "Welcome to the club!" And I am sure that any normal person would understand why I might have been prompted to do that. There simply are times when we need to get quietened *from* so much of what is incessantly going on around us. "Coming unglued"—the radical phrase that refers to the all too common feeling that we are being pressed by just too many things all at once, and that frazzled ends are sticking out all over us—makes us aware of how much we need some renewed sense of interiority. And it is then that we need to find some calm, some inner source of composure and strength, to refresh us and re-equip us for the demands and challenges and opportunities of living.

One such source that has been a constant basis of help and blessing for many is a statement of hope and confidence found in the Book of Psalms. In one place the psalmist writes something that applies to any pilgrim on a journey towards becoming who finds himself or herself suffering dryness or staleness or burnout or letdown because of the draining and fatiguing demands of life's pressures. What such a person needs is something to compose and undergird and refresh him or her. What such a person needs is a space of strengthening *quiet*, within which to get it all back together and get himself or herself refocused. And in that kind of setting I find these words of an inwardly breathed prayer of trust most helpful: "Thou shalt make (me) to drink of the river of Thy pleasure. For with Thee is the fountain of life" (Psalm 36:8,9 KJV). What a declaration of possibility and hope! It declares that there is a wellspring of refreshing, renewing, re-invigorating grace to which we can resort, and from which we can draw, that will regenerate and revivify us for the journey of life. If we can just get ourselves withdrawn from the clamor and confusion around us, we can drink from a fountain that is at the very deeps of our person, indeed, that is in the very territory of eternity, in the very presence of God, and find ourselves made fresh and strong and whole as we do.

Sometimes There Is A Quieting TO

There is more to a therapeutic experience of *quiet* than simply turning off or escaping from outer noise and distraction. It's one thing to tune *out* from the world's clamorous Babel. It's another thing to the tune *in* to a more profound and meaningful frequency within our souls. In this kind of experience we are using our minds to center down and focus in. We are not seeking for something outside ourselves to stimulate us, or hoping for something external to us to be laid on us. We are, rather, waiting for something profoundly interior to awaken within us and integrate us and illuminate us as we are open to it and are willing to be addressed by it. Whether we recognize this only dimly as our deep unconsciousness or subconsciousness; whether we reach out more particularly to affirm it as our innermost and truest selves; or whether we perceive it even more accurately in biblical terms as the voice and power of God within us, we are aware in confronting this that we are being ministered to by it, and nurtured by it, only as we turn away from exteriority to find it or let it find us. "The human spirit," the Bible declares, "is the lamp of the Lord, searching every inmost part" (Proverbs 20:27). That only happens when we are *quiet* and inwardly sensitive to that powerful, and informing, and transforming inwardness. And this can find elucidation and confirmation through a consideration of a very ancient and yet powerfully meaningful pursuit.

I refer to the science—or, as some would prefer to say, the *pre-science*—of alchemy, that arcane practice of those mysterious researchers of the middle ages who spent their time in experiments that they hoped would lead them to "the philosopher's stone"—a wonderful entity that was supposed to have the power to transmute base metals, such as lead, into the precious metal, gold. Well, no one ever found or was able to develop the philosopher's stone. But the premise behind that stone's transforming power captured the imagination of certain philosophers who moved their search away from the literal over into the realm of the metaphysical, engaging, then, in a search for some *truth* or *understanding* that would transform and ennoble the human spirit, enabling it to reach its ultimate attainment of being.

Now, one needs to understand this reference to alchemy not as an endorsement of some kind of pre-scientific world-view but simply as the illustrative employment of an ancient concept that is imbued with helpful meaning. That's why the philosophers moved from the realm of the physical to the realm of the spiritual in their quest for the transforming entity. The transformation symbolized by the transmuting effect of alchemy is one that addresses us at the very center of our being. In the realm of mind, or spirit, or soul, it is truly the very thing that we seek as we pursue the goal of newness and wholeness. And we can find it—not as such a tangible thing as the philosopher's stone, but as a spiritual thing which is the Gospel of God's grace. But in order to find it we must withdraw from the bombardment of outer distraction, and turn our selves inward to attain a quiet and receptive state. We need to be most sensitive to the life-giving and life-enhancing grace and power of God in order for any kind of radical transformation to occur in our own personal quest for meaning and becoming. Do you remember the story in the New Testament of how a woman who had suffered extremely for years from a debilitating physical condition came up to Jesus in a crowd as He was passing by, seeking healing from the affliction, which had oppressed her for so long? She reached out silently and hopefully, hesitantly and almost covertly, and managed to touch just the hem of our Lord's robe. Immediately, Jesus stopped and turned and asked, "Who touched Me?" because, we are told, He knew that power had passed from Him to some seeking soul. The woman came forth to confess what she had done, and Jesus virtually pronounced a benediction on her: "Go in peace: your faith has saved you" (see Matthew 9:20-22;Mark 5:24-34; Luke 8:42-48). Oh! that such might be the experience of each one of us, even as it was in a demonstration of grace that was expressed later, as Matthew tells it, when people brought many persons to Jesus in order that they might touch the hem of His garment, with the result being: "All who touched Him were healed" (Matthew 14:34-36.) Oh! that the renewing and transforming power of the Risen Lord might be realized in our deepest souls, that we might be transformed ourselves to be set on our way henceforth as *becomers,* gifted with the power and direction of God!

Sometimes There Is A Quieting OF

Sometimes the quiet that we seek is something very practical and personal. This is not a quieting *from,* or a quieting *to,* but a quieting *of* our own selves—of our own thoughts, words and pronouncements, including a quieting of our own unspoken judgments and criticisms that are too often formulated in our minds. Of all the lessons that we as inter-relating social beings might have learned over the long course of our human experience, surely a primary one is that words once spoken can not be recalled, and that ill thoughts toward other persons are toxic in their effect and tend to poison and harm the thinker more than they do the receiver. And yet it is a lesson that we still struggle with on a constant basis; and we will continue to do so until we determinedly commit ourselves to learn the lesson of appropriately silencing our words and checking our propensity to inner censoriousness. Words can hurt and burn and cripple and destroy without ever making a mark on the outside of one's body. No wonder the Book of Proverbs, in its expressed wisdom, asserts: "Death and life are in the power of the tongue" (Proverbs 18:21). And in the light of that, no wonder that the psalmist prays fervently in one place: "Set a guard over my mouth, O Lord; keep watch over the door of my lips" (Psalm 141:3). Well might each and every one of us so plead, in order that there may be a quieting of the all too frequent negative remarks and comments that we are so prone to offer. Surely every one of us has found at one time or another that an apology for, or even a retraction of, some judgment that we have leveled—while serving to set the record officially straight—has nonetheless fallen woefully short of truly making matters right. Better by far would it have been to accomplish an earlier quieting of those remarks—better for the person against whom they may have been uttered, and better for us in the deepest chambers of our beings where we must acknowledge that we have lost ground in our personal hopes for becoming full and gracious individuals. And the same may be said of ungracious and negative inner judgments. These, too, are often harmful to more than just a casual degree. Derogatory or denunciatory thoughts, given free rein due to umbrage, jealousy or resentment, can deeply color our estimation of another person and lessen our ability to ultimately respect and appreciate him or her, as well as casting a pall of ashamedness over our own spirits for having harbored and nurtured uncharitable notions or ideas. An ancient prayer dating from the sixteenth century offers a number of petitions well suited to growth towards becoming a worthy and effective person. Two phrases in particular from that prayer are worth noting. They ask simply: "God be in my mouth and in my speaking; God be in my heart and in my thinking."[3] When those petitions are answered, we will surely realize a gracious and fulfilling rising above unworthy and inappropriate expressions in thought and deed. This will result in an expression of charity which we ourselves are able to author and effect. And it will be all the more the characteristic expression of who and what we are as we learn to draw from the inner springs of refreshment that are ours through being silent to the clamor around us and open to the depths within us. Thus, another step on our journey to becoming is charted out before us. Sometimes, it is vital to note, all you have to do is be *quiet*.

Notes

1 "Thou Shalt Know Him When He Comes:" anonymous, c.1500.

2 "God Be in My Head," anonymous, from "The Book of Hours," c. 1514.

Chapter 18
All You Have To Do Is Be
RESILIENT

Intrepid Adventurer #1: "Uh-oh. It looks like we're going to have to go to Plan B."
Intrepid Adventurer #2: "What's Plan B?"
Intrepid Adventurer #1: "That's where we make it up as we go along."

"The best laid plans o' mice and men gang aft agley," wrote Robbie Burns,[1] in words that stress the fact that for most of us, life seems frequently and disconcertedly to be lived on the flexible border between "Plan A" and "Plan B." Changing circumstances, unforeseen developments and unexpected twists and turns regularly confront us; and we find ourselves having to alter directions, switch gears, or in some other way accommodate ourselves to a new reality. Oh! If only we could just get life to where we want it, and then freeze-frame it there, things would go much more smoothly and agreeably! But life is not like that. Life is much less fixed and much more fluid than we might like.

Jesus addressed that reality once in some words of wisdom that provide a helpful and insightful perspective on the vagaries and variations of life that we all encounter:

> "No one pours new wine into old wineskins. If he does, the wine will burst the skins, and both the wine and the wineskins will be ruined. No, he pours new wine into new wineskins" (Mark 2:2).

In using that figure of speech, Jesus wasn't just talking about preserving the current year's production from the local vineyard. He may more accurately be said to have been talking about the circumstances surrounding moving from Plan A to Plan B in our journey of life. Consider the scenario, set in a day when wine was stored in animal skins and not in glass bottles. The old wineskins that Jesus refers to would have lost their elasticity; they would be unpliable to the point of being brittle and even fragile; and to try to store fresh wine in such vessels would be both foolish and hazardous. The new wine would still possess the life and movement of fermentation, and in its agitation would require freedom for expanding and contracting. The only safe procedure would be to put that wine into flasks or skins that were, themselves, still fresh and pliable. Otherwise, the fermentation process would prove more than the old, dry skins could handle; and the life of the wine would virtually erupt through the brittleness of the flasks, with the result that everything—skins and wine together—would be lost.

New wine can be understood as a symbol for new ideas and new experiences and new situations. And the most important "skins" that we can imagine are not the animal skins used to make flasks to contain wine in New Testament days, but our own skins within which we live and move and have our being! Are detours and/or apparent dead ends too much for us to handle? Are we so stuck in the mud that we have no maneuverability, no possibility for realigning or adjusting our thinking in order to handle the unplanned and the unforeseen? The answers we provide to such queries will indicate the alternatives that are open to us. If we respond with a fixed rigidity of mind and spirit, then we acknowledge ourselves as "old skins"—not old in terms of years, necessarily, but old in the sense of being unable to respond to and welcome newness itself. And if that is the case, then we had better be prepared, sadly, to miss out on the experience of "new wine" in our lives. We'd better just be resigned to stick with the old, flat wine of what has always been, and forget about moving on in our lives to the discovery and even the conquering of new and more glorious vistas. But if we can respond affirmatively to the challenge of life as a fermenting and transforming kind of experience, then, as "skins" ready and able to adjust and to be *resilient,* we will be open to the possibilities of newness that we will encounter.

Resilience EMBRACES EXPERIENCE—"Take Your Best Shot!"

Resilience is not afraid to see the comfort and the familiarity of the *status quo* challenged, shaken, and even overthrown. The *resilient* person, indeed, is ready to face options and alternatives without trying to hide from the fact that so often and in so many ways, "the old order changeth, yielding place to new, and God fulfills Himself in many ways, lest one good custom should corrupt the world."[2]

Imagine, if you can, a baby chick, still in the egg, in the ineluctable process of being born. And imagine further that that baby chick is endowed with the faculty of reasoned observation and is able to consciously enter into the unfolding procedure of hatching in which he/she/it is at the center. What would we think, if we were able to observe everything that was happening, if that chick were to determine to prevent its snug, secure, stable world—the only world it has ever known!—from literally disintegrating around it? What would we think if we could see that chick desperately working to repair those ominous cracks in the roof of its world, frantically endeavoring to patch up the widening fracture in the shell around it? That sort of action could undoubtedly seem appropriate and even necessary to the chick, from its limited perspective and in keeping with its limited perception; but would we not assert, from our understanding of the whole process of *becoming* that that kind of action was not only not in the chick's best interests, but that it was positively destructive of the very life that the chick was trying to save? Far better, we would say, would be the approach that acknowledges the inevitability of the change that is occurring and does not try to deny it or prevent it, but capitalizes on it for the purposes of further growth and discovery and fulfillment. And, if one might imagine even further—even to the point of whimsy—one might then picture that chick as boldly and deliberately applying beak and claw to the crumbling shell around him/her/itself, and saying, even as the old structure falls away before it, and something new and unknown looms all around it: "Okay, life—if this is how it's going to be, count me in on whatever comes next. Take away everything that has been my security; threaten me with everything I don't know;—*throw whatever you've got at me!* And then, make room for me; because, no matter what, I'm a player!"

Well, that little scenario is highly imaginative, but its point is anything but far-fetched. In fact, most of us have probably felt at one time or another, that that story could actually be autobiographical! We have all faced changes—some of them pleasant and desirable, some of them tragic and devastating. There can be something exhilarating about certain kinds of changes and developments because we recognize them as offering to us the potential for personal growth; while, of course, there is nothing upbeat or positive or even the least bit welcome about some other life changes that we encounter. But face those changes—of all kinds, good or bad—we must. The shell cracks and disintegrates around us, and, like the chick, we are thrust out into a new set of circumstances and possibilities. And the unpliant, rigidly fixed person is unprepared for the swirling movement of change that so peremptorily addresses him or her. Only the *resilient* person is able to accommodate himself or herself to the new dimensions that life has suddenly taken on. Only the *resilient* person is ready to embrace any and every experience and live it through. Carrying the idea of challenge and change to its furthest point, someone has observed that the only truly settled and unchallenged person is the one lying horizontal in a satin-lined box with a lily on his or her chest. Let's face it; the way of rigidity and inflexibility is not one that offers us much sense of anticipation or possibility; and its ultimate way of being is not attractive.

Resilience EMBODIES RESOLVE—"I Will Not Be Beaten!"

According to an old adage, there are two ways to get to the top of an oak tree. One is to take hold of the tree and climb it. The other is to find an acorn and sit on it. Both ways, it seems to me, show a commendable degree of innovativeness, plus an appropriate degree of *resilience* that embodies resolve. If you've got the time, and if the opportunity presents itself, it sounds like a smart game-plan to ensconce yourself on that acorn and simply ride the natural process of change to the top. But if, as is more frequently and more realistically the case, you don't have the enviable luxury of simply riding a convenient acorn, you have to be ready to think and act decisively in order to accommodate yourself to unfolding reality. One does not simply say, "The tree is so tall and I am so small, and so I can't deal with the prospect of getting to the top." Nor does one sit idly or ineptly by in the vain hope that somebody bigger and stronger will come along and cut down that nasty, inconvenient tree, or at least turn it into a more surmountable stump. Rather, one simply determines that if the tree needs to be scaled, then, by whatever means may prove handy or best, not only am I going to make it to the top of this tree; I am also—from the vantage point attained there—proudly going to wave the banner of my own realized achievement, and say for all the world to hear, "*I will not be beaten!*"

Norman Cousins, probably best known because of his remarkable display of personal resilience chronicled in several of his books and attested to in his life and career following a deadly illness and a devastating heart attack, was for a number of years the distinguished editor of the prestigious magazine, *The Saturday Review.* In one place in his book *The Healing Heart* he writes a chapter dealing with his response to the crippling and potentially life-ending heart attack that he had suffered, and he titles that chapter very meaningfully—with a pun fully intended—"*Counterattack.*"The attitude displayed even in the choice of that title itself speaks volumes about the author's gritty determination both to endure and to prevail. It's a wonderfully appropriate use of a term because it asserts and displays the undaunted spirit of counter-offensive with which Cousins addressed his life situation. In that chapter he reveals something of the incredible ability that he possessed to deal with and handle even seemingly catastrophic change; and in one little introductory aside he indicates something about his general attitude towards life that underlay and supported his resolve and his resiliency. Thus:

> The description of *The Saturday Review* that pleased me most during the years of my editorship was that it never tried to gloss over the seriousness of the issues it discussed, but at the same time it never wavered in its belief that solutions were within reach.[3]

The kind of resolve pictured there is a necessary and integral part of the resiliency that we need in our search for full personhood. It is a reflection of the wise adage that simply says, "Things turn out in the best way for those who make the best of the way things turn out." It is a determined commitment to the spirit of never throwing in the towel, never saying "die," and never caving in or chickening out.

That sounds a tremendous note of *resilience*, arising from an iron resolve: if you won't quit, you can't be beaten.

Resilience EXPRESSES RENASCENCE—"Always Springing Up To Newness"

A homely anecdote can be instructive in this regard. A father walks out into the back yard where his six-year-old son is practicing by himself with a bat and ball. "Hey, Dad!" the boy calls; "take a look at the world's greatest slugger." So saying, the boy tosses the ball up in the air, and as it comes down, takes a murderous swing at it—and misses. "Wait a second, Dad!" the boy says, and goes through the exercise again, shouting as he swings, "Here's the world's greatest slugger!" Once more he misses. Still undaunted, he tries again—"Hang on Dad! Watch the world's greatest slugger!"—and he misses for the third time. Totally unfazed, the lad drops the bat, picks up the ball, holds it exultantly in his hand as he turns to his father with a thrilled smile on his face, and says, "Well, whatta ya know! The world's greatest pitcher!"

The one recurring message of the Bible as the record of God's dealings with humanity and God's action on behalf of humanity, is that there lies before us always the hope and challenge and possibility of something new and promising in life—"a crown of beauty instead of ashes, the oil of gladness instead of mourning, and a garment of praise instead of a spirit of despair" (Isaiah 61:2)—(maybe even the designation "the world's greatest pitcher" instead of "the world's greatest slugger!) At any rate, the Bible would seek to tell us that always, out of darkness comes light, out of lostness comes discovery, and out of death comes life. Thus, as *resilient* persons, we are open to the experience of renascence—the recovering and renewing of vigor and purpose and life, even after failure, setback and defeat. Life may change because of things that happen around us or to us. Sickness, the failure or deceit of other persons, acts of violence, acts of a seemingly random and hurtful sort, may all combine to affect us adversely and bring us to that place where we feel tapped out, trodden under foot and simply "totaled." But God's plan is that there is no place of final washout, wipeout and certainly not wimp out. We can always find the possibility to spring back—in our spirits, and thus in our deepest persons—to newness of outlook and fresh determination. And this is so not just because we can grit our teeth and come out on top through our own innate capability, but because we have a depth of resource that is able to supply us and infuse us and renew us in the time and place of need. St. Paul puts it this way: "Not that we are sufficient of ourselves to think anything as of ourselves; but our sufficiency is of God" (2Corinthians 3:5 KJV). "I can do all things through Christ which strengtheneth me" (Philippians 4:13 KJV).

The one sure place of inner refreshment and *resilience*, leading to a gracious renascence of enthusiasm and purpose, is in the feeding of the soul on the promise and power of God. "Taste and see that the Lord is good; blessed is the man who trusts in Him"(Psalm 34:8).

I do not want to sound insensitive or undiscerning, and I do not want to minimize the depth of pain and loss and despair that can accompany some of the crushing and disappointing things that happen in life. Not everything that happens to hurt us or frustrate us can be dismissed with a toss of the head and a happy little cliché. That's not the cavalier kind of thing that I would recommend. But I do believe that by the grace of God we can act as *resilient* persons and truly express renascence in our living as we spring again and again into newness of purpose and determination in our living. Thus, we find the Psalmist affirming both confidently and hopefully, "All my fresh springs are in Thee" (Psalm 87:7 BCP). I like to think that those "springs" by which God refreshes and renews us are not only springs of living water from which we may drink for our inner rejuvenation; but some sort of symbolic coil springs that we have attached to the soles of our shoes, as well—springs that bounce us up into vigorous advancement and action with a tremendous *boing!* of God-given energy and enthusiasm, and that thereby characterize and demonstrate our undeniable *resiliency*.

Notes

[1] Robert Burns, 1759-1796, "To A Mouse, On Turning Up Her Nest With The Plough," 1785.

[2] From Alfred, Lord Tennyson, 1809-1892, *The Passing of Arthur,* 1869.

[3] Norman Cousins, *The Healing Heart* (New York: W.W. Norton & Company, 1983) p.72.

Chapter 19
All You Have To Do Is Be
SPIRIT-FILLED

"Be filled with the Spirit" (Ephesians 5:18).

The first thing to be made utterly clear in speaking of being *Spirit-filled* as a part of our quest for personal fulfillment and becoming is that this does not in any way simply represent an option that will improve our performance, as though we will thereby be made more dynamic and efficient in our living. The Holy Spirit is the sovereign Lord, not some kind of merely functional quality that can be added on to or added in to our personalities simply in order to make them and us more nearly optimal in daily operation. He is not some kind of desirable extra that we can select in our search for the highest and best expression of our humanity—a sort of turbo option for one's inner self, to provide more pickup, pizzazz and punch, more zip, zowie and zing, along the road of human experience. To subscribe to that notion would be to presume that God is somehow simply at our disposal, for us to incorporate Him into our plans and our agenda because we can use Him. We need to realize, rather, that to be Spirit-Filled is to be in a reverent relationship with the almighty and eternal God that involves the dimensions of repentance, confession, and humble submission. It does not involve *our* coming to possess anything extra or extra-special at all. It involves *God* coming to possess some *one,* namely *you* and/or *me,* in a certain special way, which is a way of totality and sovereignty. Apropos of which consider two illustrative references.

One is a story about a little boy who was engaging in some theological speculation one day as he and his mother were sitting at the breakfast table. "Mother," the boy asked, "is it true that God is everywhere?" "Yes," his mother assured him; "God is everywhere." "Is He in this room right now?" the boy continued. "Yes," his mother said again, "He is here in this room right now." The boy considered that for a moment, and then, very reflectively—taking the matter a logical step further—asked yet another question. "Well," he wanted to know, pointing to the sugar container on the table in front of him, "is God here in this sugar bowl?" The mother wasn't quite sure where this was leading, but again she answered in the affirmative. "Yes," she replied; "God is there in the sugar bowl." Whereupon the young lad then quickly shot out his hand, slapped it over the top of the sugar bowl, and, sealing the bowl thereby, cried out exultantly, "I got Him! I got Him!" All of which might seem merely somewhat bizarre and not particularly relevant, except for a pertinent biblical account which addresses the principle involved there.

In the eighth chapter of the book of Acts we find recorded the story of Simon the Magician, a man apparently skilled in the practice of sorcery and conjuration of some sort. People listened to him eagerly, the record says, and had done so for years, "because for a long time he had amazed them with his magic." Then, Philip the evangelist came into town preaching the redemptive message of Jesus; and many people believed and experienced a life-changing transformation as a result, which impressed Simon tremendously. Moreover, his impression was deepened to an even greater degree when Peter and John came along and confirmed the new converts in their faith by laying hands upon them; because when that happened, those converts "received the Holy Spirit" and were even more overtly and pronouncedly affected. This obviously represented an endowment unlike anything that Simon had ever seen before. And this prompted a further response in him, not entirely unlike that of the little boy with the sugar bowl.

> Then Peter and John laid their hands on them, and they received the Holy Spirit. Now, when Simon saw that the Holy Spirit was given through the laying on of the Apostles' hands, he offered them money, saying, "Give me also this power, so that anyone on whom I lay my hands may receive the Holy Spirit." But Peter said to him, "May your silver perish with you, because you thought you could obtain God's gift with money! You have no part or share in this, for your heart is not right before God. Repent, therefore, of this wickedness of yours, and pray to the Lord that, if possible, the intent of your heart may be forgiven you. For I see that you are in the gall of bitterness and the chains of wickedness." Simon answered, "Pray for me to the Lord, that nothing of what you have said may happen to me" (Acts 8:17-24).

Simon learned quickly and painfully that God's Spirit is not an instrumental entity that can be gotten or given through human intention or ingenuity. You can't line people up and promise to dole out to them the gift of the Holy Spirit, as though He were some kind of commodity. So, how, then, are we to understand the injunction with which this chapter began—"Be filled with the Spirit"? What are the parameters within which we may grasp what it means to receive and know the fullness of the Spirit of God?

The Holy Spirit Underlies And Pervades All Of Human Life

We begin by noting the basic fact that there is no life that is not life from the Spirit of God. He is "the Lord, the Giver of life." No one lives anywhere apart from the gracious aegis of the One whose presence alone imbues all with the gift of being.

> The Lord God formed man from the dust of the ground, and breathed into his nostrils the breath of life—(*i.e.*, the spirit of life—the word for "spirit" and the word for "breath" are the same word in the original language)—and the man became a living being (Genesis 2:7).

Thus, at the very least it may be observed that, while the Holy Spirit may sometimes seem to be a stranger to us, yet we are not strangers to Him. We are here in the first place because of Him; we are not, in fact, self-originating. We did not spring into being through the determination of our own will; we are here because of God's inspiration, literally, because of God's "in-Spirit-ation." God is "the God of the spirits of all flesh" (Numbers 16:22). He is "the Lord who stretched out the heavens and founded the earth and formed the human spirit within" (Zechariah 12:1). We live by the grace of the Spirit of God. All persons do.

To have life from the Spirit of God as the most elemental factor of our existence is simply something that is a given reality for every person. It is not as though we might say, even on a basis of outright atheism, "I do not choose to have any dealings with the Holy Spirit." That sounds impressively self-assertive, but it's an utter impossibility. It can't be done. To say, "I do not accept life from the Spirit of God," is about as viable as saying, "I have decided not to breathe during my lifetime." That can't be done either. And it's definitely not smart to try it! Thus the psalmist asks:

> Where can I go from Your Spirit? Or where can I flee from Your presence? If I ascend to heaven, You are there; if I make my bed in the grave, You are there. If I take the wings of the morning and settle at the farthest limits of the sea, even there Your hand shall lead me, and Your right hand shall hold me fast (Psalm 139:7-10).

There just isn't any place where God isn't, including with, around and in us.

The Holy Spirit Judges and Heals The Brokenness Of Human Life

It is foundational to understand that we all have life through the Holy Spirit. But the New Testament is obviously talking about something much more pointed, something much more personally transforming and empowering, than elemental Spirit-given existence in its references to the redeeming and galvanizing fullness of God's Spirit. And this something comes about as a result of the Lordship of Jesus being realized and confessed in anyone's life. Then we not only have life *from* and *by* the Spirit, but life *in* and *through* the Spirit—indeed, the very life *of* the Spirit. And that is what makes the difference in our living in the world and turns our existence into *being* and *becoming*. And that is where we come to address the matter of being "filled" with the Spirit.

We need to remember always that the gift of the Spirit is life. And *life* is what we need. Basic, existent life is necessary for our physical living. Take a dead body and do what you will cosmetically and circumstantially to it or with it and you still will have only a corpse on your hands. Only life will suffice to give meaning to that body. And the same is true spiritually. We have been made alive in Christ, through the power of the Spirit, St. Paul declares (Colossians 2:13). Now we need to let that life manifest itself in us. And as that happens, we will find ourselves being both humbled and lifted up, both convicted and encouraged.

First, we face the Spirit's *judgment*. And then we receive the Spirit's *healing* and *empowerment*. This relates to the essence of who we are before God. We are creatures of dust, flawed and imperfect in our ways, in our attitudes, and even in our longings and desires; and that is how we present ourselves before the God of burning perfectness and holiness, the One who is "of purer eyes than to countenance iniquity" (Habakkuk 1:13). "Behold, now, I, who am but dust and ashes, have taken it upon me to speak to the Lord" (Genesis 18:27 KJV). Well may we then be humbled before Him, as He searches and judges our sinfulness and our brokenness.

But observe further—very importantly—that there is a great deal of difference between genuine humility, which is appropriate for us and which God receives and approves; and groveling self-abjuration, which is demeaning and out of place for us and which God in no way requires or enjoys. In no way is our attitude intended to be one that denies the dignity of our stature as persons made in the image of God and given breath and spirit by the decree of God. In true and reverent biblical humility there ought not to be any assumed quality of woebegone vileness, and no element of utter self-loathing—only an acknowledgement of the infinite greatness and splendor of our God, before which we quite naturally and unquestionably pale into abysmally finite imperfection and brokenness. But, notwithstanding, this is not to underestimate God's love for us nor to disesteem God's evaluation of us. We are the work of His hands and the joy of His creation, and we must never forget that. But He is the sovereign and most high God; and we must never forget *that,* either. We truly are created "just a little lower than the angels," and have been "crowned with glory and honor" (Psalm 8:5 KJV). But, just as truly, when we address ourselves to the almighty and most holy person of God, our response must be that of Job: "I had heard of You by the hearing of the ear, but now my eye sees You; therefore I despise myself, and repent in dust and ashes" (Job 42:5-6).

The Holy Spirit Transfigures And Intensifies The Quality Of Human Life

The fullness of the Holy Spirit is a gracious Christian doctrine that holds up for us the ideal of what old-time Methodism described as "going on to perfection"—the ever-increasing realization of God's intention for us in every area of our lives. Essentially, that is of course what this entire book is about, as we consider together some of the areas wherein we may realize something more of what it can mean to become the persons we are called to be. But being Spirit-Filled as the *sine qua non* of aspiring personhood is not as simple as it sounds. In fact, it has become a rather clouded and complex matter, involving various doctrinal considerations that have turned it into a rather forbidding bit of theological esoterica difficult for the average person to grasp and even more difficult for the average person to simply take and experience. That's unfortunate; because, after all, the New Testament asserts that Christians experienced the fullness of the Holy Spirit as a gracious gift from God long before there was any doctrinal formulation to box it in, or fence it off, or sew it up. And the focal point of that experience was, from earliest times, the same as it is now: confession and experience of Jesus the Lord as the One in whom we find life. When our relationship to Jesus as Lord parallels Jesus' relationship to God in terms of utter commitment, yieldedness, trust and obedience, then we share in the life and fullness of the Spirit even as Jesus participated in the life and Spirit of His Father. God's grace comes to us in the person and message of Jesus. If we want to receive God and the fullness of life that He offers we simply need to open ourselves to the truth of Christ, accept Him and embrace Him as our Lord, and offer our hearts fully to Him. That's all we have to do. That's all we *can* do. God does the rest. Through His living Spirit He effects the work of His grace in our lives, and we are made new through the action of the Holy Spirit. We do not need to seek the Spirit of Life, for He has already sought and found us. All we have to do is live so that we do not hamper or lessen His unfolding work within us and through us. We are told not to "grieve" the Holy Spirit (Ephesians 4:30), and not to "quench" His work in us (1 Thessalonians 5:19). We are, rather, instructed to "walk according to" the Holy Spirit (Galatians 5:16). And if we do that, we will not need to be constantly fretting about whether or not we are "filled" with the Spirit, for that state of fullness is nothing more or less than the state of full yieldedness to the Lordship of Jesus and faithfulness to Him. The person-enriching power and purity of the Holy Spirit are ours not because we attain to some quantitative level of possession but because we are truly more and more open to the qualitative realization of God's presence within us.

St. Paul sets out two catalogs of human characteristics that underline the importance of simply being in the place where God, the Holy Spirit, can set our hearts and lives on fire with the grace of Jesus the Lord. Paul lists first what he calls "the works of the flesh"—a compendium of negative and destructive personality traits that we would acknowledge as anything but "good," including such things as "fornication, impurity, licentiousness, jealousy, anger, quarrels, factions, envy and drunkenness" (Galatians 5:19-21). But then Paul speaks of what he calls "the fruit of the Spirit"—positive and uplifting virtues which lead to fullness of being and becoming to the glory of God, such as "love, patience, kindness, generosity, faithfulness, gentleness and self-control" (Galatians 5:22-24). He then says simply, and definitively, "Let us be guided by the Spirit" (verse 25). And as long as your heart is truly made the place where Jesus Christ lives and rules as Lord, you will be led and empowered by His Spirit; for you will be filled with that Spirit as the empowering, life-enhancing dynamic of your very being.

I remember being approached once, a number of years ago now, by a young lady who was a member of the congregation which I served as minister. She said that she wished to discuss a problem with me, and so we arranged a time to meet. At our meeting she then set out before me her difficulty; which was that, even though she was a church member and attended services regularly and sang in the choir, she did not know how she should think of or understand the person and place of the Holy Spirit in her life. Each week in our worship we sang the Gloria Patri:

> Glory be to the Father, and to the Son,
> And to the Holy Ghost.
> As it was in the beginning, is now and ever shall be,
> World without end, Amen.

Those were just words to her, and beyond whatever acknowledgement of the Holy Spirit's person and role they contained, as far as she could see the Holy Spirit was not evident anywhere else in her life.

Well, this phase of our quest for fullness of person is not meant to bog us down in theological profundities; and as significant as it might be to digress at this point into a consideration of the doctrine of the Holy Spirit in particular and the Holy Trinity in general, and as much as I might recommend that to the reader in another setting, I want to zero in on the simple reality that underlies our journey to becoming. To that end, I say again what I stated just a few paragraphs earlier: "As long as your heart is truly made the place where Jesus Christ lives and rules as Lord, you will be led and empowered by His Spirit; for you will be filled with that Spirit as the empowering, life-enhancing dynamic of your very being."

"Be filled with the Spirit." Don't view that as a *command,* in response to which we must scramble around in an attempt to comply with its directive. Rather, see it as an *invitation* to be utterly open and submissive to the presence of God and the power and peace and purity that come as He dwells with us and in us.

Chapter 20
All You Have To Do Is Be
TRUSTING

One of the most famous of all books having to do with the movement and growth of the person towards ultimate wholeness of being is the extended allegory, *Pilgrim's Progress,* by John Bunyan.[1] Bunyan's beautiful story is one of the great accomplishments of English literature in general and one of the great examples of the literature of personal piety in particular, and a reading of that work can prove to be both helpful and inspiring. It can also be both illustrative and instructive, particularly with regard to the part of our subject that we address in this chapter.

At one juncture in the symbolic journey of the book's main character, all "progress" comes to a halt when Pilgrim and his traveling companion, Hopeful, are taken prisoner, flung into a dungeon, and left to languish forlornly there. They are effectively stopped in their movement towards the goal to which they feel God is calling them. They can go no further, and they have to face the dispiriting fact that if they cannot manage somehow to free themselves from the bondage they are in, their journey will end at this point in frustration and failure. They can see no way out. It looks as if everything is finished for them. And their plight is emphasized with true allegorical appropriateness through the name of the place to which they have been consigned and the name of the guard who holds them prisoner. They have gotten into trouble in the first place because they have entered "Doubting Castle;" and the guard there, who is determined that they shall never escape, is a grim giant named "Despair." So they settle down into a deep resignation of lostness and despondency, even to the point of enduring such misery and distress that all day long "they spent their time in nothing but sighs and bitter lamentations." It is assuredly worth reading about them to discover how they finally were able to use the key called "Promise" to get themselves free; but I leave the story there. Rather than following through on the classical allegory of Pilgrim's Progress, I would like to extrapolate from the single reference I have made to it a concern regarding the present reality of our own progress towards wholeness, by considering something that can serve as a powerful and effective antidote to the whole syndrome of doubting and despair and the all too real sense of futility and despondency that accompanies it. Here we learn the lesson and the necessity of being *trusting*.

Being Trusting Can Be LONELY And FRIGHTENING

Freda Hanbury Allen has written some enlightening words:

> Trust were not trust, if thou couldest see
> The ending of the way;
> Nor couldest thou learn God's songs by night,
> Were life one radiant day.[2]

Well, "not to worry," as they say—because the possibility of being able to "see the ending of the way," in the sense of being able to confidently fathom where life is going when you're in the midst of confusion or sorrow or pain, is pretty slight. And the prospect of experiencing life as "one radiant day" has even less likelihood of occurrence. Rather, very much the opposite seems to be the lot of most ordinary, struggling human beings. In fact, some words from the Psalmist may be understood as more nearly representing the kind of experience that most of us frequently have to struggle with and fumble through:

> How long, O Lord? Will You forget me forever? How long will You hide Your face from me? How long must I wrestle with my thoughts, and have sorrow in my heart? (Psalm 13:1-2).

Every one of us, it seems, will have ample opportunity to "learn God's songs by night," in the darkness of less than ideal settings—to try to discover the meaning and purpose of our Creator's design and intent for us against a background of uncertainty and unpropitiousness. We'll get lots of practice in walking where we don't know where we're going, and of feeling our way along in the dark. And that's where the attitude of being *trusting* comes into play. "The best defense is a good offence," they say. And trust is a most powerful weapon to wield against the forces of doubt and despair. Apropos of which, this.

There is something that I have wondered about for a long time now—something having to do with a housing subdivision in certain city that I know. This subdivision happened to have been built in an area adjacent to a golf and country club; and the golf club motif was noticeable, not only in the lush green lawns and splendid views surrounding the homes but even in the names of some of the streets. Certainly that's not unusual, and that's not what I've always wondered about. I have lived in other centers where there were thoroughfares bearing such names as "Fairway Road," and "Putting Green Lane" and the like; but never anywhere except this one particular town where there was actually a street that bore the name "Stymie Boulevard"—and that's what has always caused me to wonder. Why would any subdivision developer—who must have wanted to appeal positively to prospective residents and who surely wanted to encourage people to buy a new home in a new and burgeoning area and make a new and optimistic start—name one of the streets "Stymie Boulevard"? It is, as they say, a "downer." The very name speaks loudly and clearly of pessimism and discouragement. In golf there are all kinds of terms that can be happy and positive. There's "hole-in-one," there's "eagle," and "birdie," or even "par:" so why choose a name like "stymie?" The term applies, as you may know, to a situation in which one player's ball sits on the green in a direct line between the cup and another player's ball. The player with the far ball is required by the rules to putt before the player whose ball is nearer the cup, but in this case he or she cannot, because access to the cup is completely blocked off. That's what you call a "stymie." And that term, "stymie," has passed over from the game of golf into the language of our culture, and has now come to be applied to a situation that can arise in anyone's life—a situation where difficulties so dominate and control matters that there simply appears to be no solution possible for the resolving of the predicament. To be stymied is to be so absolutely thwarted and shut off from any possibility of a happy outcome that one simply acknowledges that fact and bows to its inevitability. Oh, I know that in a game of golf, stymies can be worked around by the impeding ball being lifted and its spot marked so that the other ball may be played. (Too bad there is not some similar provision for getting around the totally blocked situations in real life!) But there just isn't. And that's why I wonder about naming a street Stymie Boulevard! But somebody did, and people actually live there. I don't know if they live there complacently, or with indifference, or perhaps with resignation and discouragement—or maybe with dauntlessness, defiance and determination!—or whether, even, some of those residents sometimes feel like getting up a petition to have the city council change the name of their street! At any rate, it must give one pause, to say the least, to wake up every morning and have to contend with living on a street whose very name spells despair! And yet, of course, as much of a factor as it would be to have to deal with living physically on Stymie Boulevard, the real problem would be to feel that one was bound to such an address in the more important realm of one's mind and spirit; because there, there really ought to be no such address. My sense of *trust* in the mercy and wisdom and kindness of God tells me that, in fact, there is no true stymie for the one who seeks to know and follow the gracious will of a good and creative God. There is always hope and meaning beyond what I can see from where I now stand. Oh, no benevolent giant hand is going to reach down and pluck me and my situation out of harm's way or lift the deadening impasse that I face—at least, not in the fairy-tale, magical way that we sometimes long for. But God by His grace will provide a way for me to cope with and handle the situation; and by trustingly walking with Him I will go on in my journey towards fullness and wholeness, despite present indications to the contrary.

Being Trusting Means Saying The Ultimate "Yes"

The ultimate "Yes" that is the essence of *trust* is not a half-hearted or reluctant "Yes," but an utter and profound *"Yes!"*—a matter of deliberately placing ourselves and all of the concerns and involvements of life into the wise and merciful care of God and believing that this is the surest and wisest move for us to make. "Let us fall into the hands of the Lord," David is reported as saying, "for His mercy is great" (2 Samuel 24:14).

The ultimate "*Yes!*" of *trust* is also something that we offer gladly, not sullenly or resentfully. We do not harbor in our hearts the secret conviction that we would rather have it some other way, and that we bow our heads to "the will of God" only because we have no other alternative.

Nor is the ultimate "*Yes!*" of *trust* an expression of defeat, with a sense of dejection pervading our spirits over what is viewed as a necessary compliance with what is regretfully seen as God's will. Rather, the ultimate *"Yes!"* of trust is an affirmation of God's wisdom, mercy and lovingkindness that gives us the assurance that even when we might have chosen or preferred that things work out differently for us, we can recognize and affirm the graciousness of God's hand in all that transpires.

Now, I do not express these thoughts lightly or easily, because I know that they contain a prescription that is strong medicine, indeed. Those words do not counsel cowardice, or dereliction of purpose. They do not advocate a sniveling, groveling self-deprecation, or masochistic self-punishment. They stand in the full light of the will to self-determination and the committed striving that must mark each person's quest for fullness and wholeness of being. But they do so in the light of an overriding faith and confidence in the goodness and fatherliness and caring love of the One whose purposes of personal fulfillment we are seeking in our journey of life. They speak of an assured willingness to receive and embrace whatever life sets out before us, or offers to us—or *slings at* us!—In the knowledge that our journey is ever forward and that God's grace and presence are our guarantee that we are able to move through and beyond anything that happens, and come out on the other side deepened and strengthened by it all. Through *trust* in the ultimate wisdom and goodness of God we can find depth and meaning and fulfillment in whatever does take place. God is never going to short-change us, but is present in anything and everything to enrich us.

Consider the following simple, rather mundane illustration, which, although seemingly unmomentous in itself, yet became for those of us involved in it a rather more profound pointer to all of life with its twists and turns and its opportunities for *trust* in every circumstance. This concerns another phase of another trip that my wife and daughter and I had the joy of making to Great Britain. We had rented a car upon our arrival, and were spending our vacation touring the country seeking out many of the seemingly countless places and points of historical and cultural interest.

It was our custom, as we traveled, to—each evening—get out the Tour Guide and the Road Atlas, and map out an itinerary for the next day, designing our trip to hit as many of the highlights as possible. One night, as we looked over the material spread before us—checking for stately manors, and castles, and gardens, and cathedrals and the like—we spotted something that just sort of jumped out at us as a point of unusual interest. It was a place with a name like no other name that we had ever seen on any map before, and it begged—you might almost say it *demanded*—some further investigation. There it was on the map, designated as—believe it or not—"Fatlips Castle"! We all agreed that we had to see that! So the next day we set out.

Now, Fatlips Castle, as it happened, was some distance away, through some rather daunting territory consisting of, as it turned out, a maze of B-Roads and Country Lanes, with twistings and turnings everywhere. But we persevered. And yet, despite our determination, and despite the fact that our Road Atlas was as up-to-date and as detailed as you could get, there nevertheless seemed to be a growing sense of elusiveness about our destination. And to top it all off, it was raining—one of those miserable, steady, drizzling rains that make traveling frequently difficult, often less than pleasant, and sometimes downright nerve-wracking. We kept on keeping on, though, because we had our hearts set on seeing Fatlips Castle. (I must confess to a secret personal agenda in this regard. I wanted to get a picture, so that I could show slides of it later, at home, while saying quite nonchalantly to anyone watching the slides, "And here we are visiting *Fatlips Castle!*")

Well, despite our best efforts that day, our search for our prized destination proved fruitless. We never did manage to find Fatlips Castle, and we ended up driving home disappointed, and defeated, and somewhat deflated. Until—just a few miles from home—the rain stopped, the clouds lifted, and the sun began to shine. And then we saw it!

Oh, not Fatlips Castle that we had had our hearts so set on, but a glorious *RAINBOW,* the likes of which we had never seen before nor have ever seen since. It stretched across the entire sky in a full-spectrum display of the richest, most intense hues imaginable, causing us to stop the car in wonder and simply to pull over to park on the shoulder, there to pause and drink in that glorious sight. I declare, that rainbow was so real, so vivid, and so almost *tangible,* that I almost thought I could have gotten out of the car, gone out into the field in front of us, to the rainbow's end, and dug up the pot of gold that would surely have been there! And at that moment what came to my mind was the awe-struck sentiment of William Wordsworth's poem:

> My heart leaps up when I behold a rainbow in the sky;
> So was it when my life began,
> So is it now I am a man,
> So be it when I shall grow old, or let me die![3]

And along with that, I couldn't help being reminded, as well, of the divine purpose expressed in the Book of Genesis concerning the symbolism of the rainbow. "I will set My bow in the clouds," God Himself is recorded as affirming, "in order to testify to my faithfulness. I make a covenant between Myself and humankind, and I seal that covenant with this sign. And what the rainbow says as My promise, and will continue to say as long as time will last, is: 'You can count on Me to uphold and sustain and shepherd all those who turn to Me in faith and trust'" (Genesis 9:12-17, paraphrased). That's an old, old promise. But it is utterly contemporary as a beautiful expression of divine constancy, whose message is eternally relevant. We three travelers missed seeing Fatlips Castle that day. Our eyes never got to behold it. But our very souls were touched with a beauty and a glory that truly surpassed and outshone our original hope by far.

The lesson for learning to *trust* is implicit. It is so easy and so commonplace for us to set our hearts on some goal in life, and give ourselves to its pursuit, in the same way that our family had set out so eagerly and purposefully for Fatlips Castle—only to find, as we found, that that goal eludes us. Our experience that day brought home to me the fact that God truly works in ways that are beyond our planning and striving, and that sometimes something quite other than what we had striven for appears as a blessing that can surprise us and enrich us and fill us with the joy of living.

Being Trusting Has Tangible Benefits and Rewards

The person who has truly resolved to live in an attitude of trust finds his or her spirit reflecting the results of that decision. When my confidence is placed to the utmost in the wisdom and graciousness of God, I am set free to expend all my psychic strength and effort in the confident pursuit of full and fulfilled personhood. My mind is not shackled with doubts about the validity of my life and my life-journey. My emotions are not crippled with misgivings about how fair or unfair life is. I can be a person of calm and hopeful demeanor because I have a sense of purpose with regard to my own life, and a sense of confidence with regard to the Power that stands behind the universe. "The people who do know their God shall be strong and do exploits" (Daniel 11:32 KJV). Without a deep sense of trust, I will walk only hesitantly and unhappily; and I will rob myself of any sense of assurance and anticipation concerning the unfolding future, with no "exploits" on the way to *becoming.* With that sense of ultimate *trust,* however, I am prepared to venture confidently and competently on my ongoing journey towards the wholeness of person that I seek.

"We are clad in the goodness of God and enclosed," says Julian of Norwich. The knowledge of that all-embracing goodness underlies the faith and confidence of every truly *trusting* soul.

Notes

1 John Bunyan, 1628-1688, *Pilgrim's Progress,* 1678.

2 Freda Hanbury Allen, "My Plans For Thee," in *Herald of Christ's Kingdom,* October, 1944, Vol.10, used by permission.

3 William Wordsworth, 1770-1850, *"The Rainbow,"* 1802.

Chapter 21
All You Have To Do Is Be

UNCONVENTIONAL

The term "conventional" can describe on the one hand a convenient and assuring way of being in the world, which we can appreciate and endorse; and on the other hand a stultifying and constricting imposition, which we very naturally view as negative. On the positive side, to be conventional means simply to accept as my own an array of already thought-out and provided beliefs and values found within our society and to follow the already laid-out path of behavior prescribed and endorsed by public agreement. There is a great body of accepted protocol and practice—some of it written, some of it unwritten—that stands as a helpful rule and guide to the way we do many things in our interactions with one another. Call it etiquette, call it a social code, call it simple civility—it all means essentially one thing: that I am able to function acceptably and efficiently in many situations and settings simply by doing many things in a prescribed and sanctioned manner, knowing that it is only as each person in society agrees to play by those rules that we can have an ordered and reliable life together as a community. And I feel better knowing that others, too, will be acting in such conventional ways. But that's only part of the matter—the good part.

There is also a dark side to being conventional—a side that is not life-enhancing but life-diminishing; a side that actually impedes my process of *becoming* by limiting me and restricting me in the truest and deepest expression of who I am, smothering the profound inner beingness that I am striving to know and express under a gray cloud of innocuous practice or contradictive custom. Sometimes convention can thwart my most sincere and most deeply held convictions and require me to think, and compel me to act, in a way that I find unrelated to my values and detrimental to my personhood. And it is this negative side of convention, that operates on the assumption that I will be willing to be less than true to myself, that I want to address and correct now. Just think of how differently the old fairy tale about The Ugly Duckling would have turned out if that duckling had knuckled under to the pressures around it and adopted a mind-set that would have consigned it to a life-long experience of feeling odd and inferior just because it was what it was! If that ugly duckling had capitulated to conventional thinking it would have ended up as nothing more than an awkwardly overgrown duck with a funny-looking neck, and it would never have realized that it could be a beautiful, graceful swan with a regal bearing. Well, that's only a fairy tale, but it does have a moral and it does teach a lesson.

Clones Belong In Science Fiction

An expression that we have all heard and used before is the one that refers to "a square peg in a round hole." It's a graphic description of a sense of conflict that most of us have felt at some time or another as we have encountered the requirement to accept what convention would dictate as our attitude or response in any given situation. "You're just not supposed to be a square peg," convention dictates. "You're just supposed to act and think like everybody else. Knock off a few corners and edges from yourself if you must, or squeeze and push a little if you prefer; but don't expect to be accommodated in any way with regard to your own peculiarity of thought or conviction. Just jump into that round hole, whether you think you're a square peg or not, and act like the round peg we want you to be." That may sound somewhat extreme, but I think it is no more than what most of us have felt reality to be on some occasion or other, with regard to some significant matter or other. It just doesn't feel right; it's a bad fit; it's an imposition of a way of thinking about things, or a way of doing things, that grates against our own convictions or persuasions. And it isn't just a case of our not having our "'druthers," or of our having to adapt our preferences or alter our expectations. We would be able to work out some way to live with that. After all, no one should expect always to have everything his or her own way in an interrelated society, and sometimes negotiation and modification and even appropriate adjustment and concession are called for in order to make things come out right for all concerned. But this is different. This is a requirement that is laid on me that sets off a disharmony within the deepest part of my being, something that I cannot accept without squelching my own real self and losing something of who I know in my heart and soul I am called to be. And very frequently this comes to focus in a requirement to *conform* in some way; to act according to the persuasion of some other person or persons; to pretend to be someone I am not, in order to "go along."

There's a simple biblical illustration of how this sort of thing crops up and how it must be handled if my own integrity of person is not to be violated. This comes from the account in the Old Testament of David's famous encounter with the giant Goliath. Everyone knows how that turned out; but what everyone may not know is that it never would have turned out that way if convention had been observed!

As this well-known story unfolds before us in the scriptures, we observe that it was really a matter of coincidence that David happened upon the scene where the Philistines and the Israelites were squared off for battle. He was actually too young to be considered for military service, and his wartime job was the unglamorous but important one of looking after his father's sheep. He had really only come to the battle front to find his older brothers, who were serving as soldiers, and to give to them some provisions that their father had sent. And he basically was just standing by, and just happened to overhear the champion Goliath defying the armies of the Lord and heaping abuse on King Saul and his men because no one would dare to come out and engage him in a one-on-one encounter. Well, David's overhearing of Goliath may have been just *accidental,* but it certainly wasn't just *incidental!* The whole thing was too much for David, who was both earnestly patriotic and intensely religious. It stung him deeply that this enemy braggart was daring to blaspheme the name of God, and it amazed him that someone from Saul's army didn't just rush headlong out to take up the challenge for the honor of God and country. And when it became apparent that every soldier there, including the redoubtable King Saul himself, was more inclined to hemming and hawing than to hurling himself into the fray, David volunteered to go against Goliath himself! And that's where *convention* came into the equation.

Because he was desperate for a volunteer, King Saul was actually willing to let the spunky shepherd boy go out there and take his chances against the giant; but this would have to be done according to certain regulations and formalities, notably with regard to proper battle attire. No matter that David's basic recommendation of himself was that he had protected his father's sheep from both lions and bears by deploying his own cunning, and that he could handle himself against formidable foes through the wiles he had developed while surviving out among the rugged and dangerous hills. No; David must dress himself up and deck himself out in the way *Saul* would have done, had *he* been going out to fight Goliath. And David must use the battle strategy that *Saul* would have used. It was the right way, the military way, and the *only* way, to proceed. And, had it been carried out, it would have proven to be also a foolish and fatal way for David. But David had sense enough and integrity enough and courage enough to break with convention and be *himself,* instead of trying to be a poor imitation of Saul.

> Saul dressed David in his own tunic. He put a coat of armor on him and a bronze helmet on his head. David fastened on his sword over the tunic and tried walking around, because he was not used to them. "I cannot go in these," he said to Saul, "because I am not used to them." So he took them off. Then he took his staff in his hand, chose five smooth stones from the stream, put them in the pouch of his shepherd's bag and, with his sling in his hand, approached the Philistine (1 Samuel 17:38-40).

It must have been something hilarious indeed to see David in the initial stages of his preparation, after he had gallantly donned Saul's battle gear! There he was, a mere callow youth, lacking in physical stature and presence, essaying to fill shoes literally many times too big for him—a medium-short, virtually swimming in the outfit of a double-X large!—with Saul's sword dragging on the ground behind him and Saul's armor bowing his legs out and Saul's helmet falling down over his eyes—giving the impression of being nothing so much as an ancient precursor of Charlie Chaplin! "But this isn't *me!*" David protested. "You're going to have to let me be *myself* here, so that I can fulfill my destiny *my* way!" And David's words and David's sentiment have echoed over the centuries since in a way that has resonated within the heart and spirit of many a person. "Never mind convention!" every integrity-driven soul would echo David. "Just because 'they' believe something to be the case, just because some peer group or even some particularly significant other person is persuaded concerning what my attitude or behavior in some specific case should be; if the armor and the sword don't fit, they will only impede my personal becoming and my personal effectiveness. I'm not trying to be a rebel, or to be contrary just for the sake of being contrary, and I certainly don't want to act half-baked or go off half-cocked; I'm just trying to fathom my own authenticity and be true to who I am. Give me my sling and my stones—they are, after all, my God-given apparatus, the means whereby I am peculiarly equipped to contend in life—and let me prove what I am able to do and be."

Very simply—as Saul's profound misjudgment of David's need for fighting apparel will witness—one size does *not* fit all.

My Individuality Is God's Gift To Me

If you use a cookie-cutter to stamp out gingerbread men, then every gingerbread man is going to look exactly like every other gingerbread man. If you use a mimeograph machine or a Xerox copier to produce printed material, then every sheet of material will be exactly like every other sheet of material. Nowhere in the Bible is there even the remotest hint that our wise Creator used mass production methods to produce human beings! Psalm 139 speaks of a much more singular and individual approach adopted by God in giving us life and purpose. "You created my inmost being; You knit me together in my mother's womb. . . . My frame was not hidden from You when I was woven together in the depths of the earth. I praise You because I am fearfully and wonderfully made" (Psalm 139:13-14). Based on the particular and detailed interest that God expresses in our creation, we cherish dearly the precious right to think our own thoughts and make our own decisions and live by our own commitments; and any encroachment upon the sacredness of our own personality is anathema to us. We want to live by the certitude of our own light. We don't want to be told that we must be like everyone else. We are not like everyone else. We are not like *anyone* else! We may not even be very much like the person that others think we are! We are growing, learning, journeying, becoming ones who cry out for the recognition of our own peculiar personhood. If we fail to claim and assert our own true self—our own distinct personhood—then we must not be surprised if someone else does that for us; in which case we will be then consigned to live, always, a despairing life which is less than that to which we are called. Life is not meant to be just one big game of "Simon Says," where we are afraid to act outside the parameters of what someone else dictates, lest we be penalized for non-conformity.

Every person can and must assert and live his or her own individuality! Even in the most restrictive and demanding of circumstances, even where our bodies are not free, our minds and spirits can still soar. No other person or persons can claim for themselves the spirit that is within us. We may be constrained to do or not to do certain things by the dictates of others who have an authority over us; but our attitude even in those circumstances can be one of grace and dignity and inner pride that declares the sanctity and the beauty of our own God-given personhood.

Is Somebody Else Pulling Your Strings?

The above question must surely provoke only one response from any person seeking personal wholeness!—namely, "Please! I'd rather do it myself! Hands off my strings!" My own individuality is just too precious to allow it to be compromised by stultifying accommodation within the strictures of convention. Therefore, I will resist being told that I must acquiesce to being simply conventional! Our very existence as viable seekers in quest of vital personhood depends upon such an unequivocal determination; which reminds me of a verse of Scripture that speaks very pointedly about the career of a certain undeniably great and truly nobly individualistic man—Moses, the hero of the story of the Exodus in the Old Testament. In recounting the story of Moses, the writer of the Book of Hebrews in the New Testament uses a very telling expression to indicate the intensity and the depth of Moses' conviction about not being manipulated in any way that would deny his own integrity.

> By faith, Moses, when he had grown up, refused to be known as the son of Pharaoh's daughter. He chose to be mistreated along with the people of God rather than to enjoy the pleasures of sin for a short time (Hebrews 11:24-25).

That sounds rather dramatic, and perhaps more extreme than the case might be with most of us. But I don't think it is extreme at all in the most realistic light of our call to self-determination. Sometimes it simply comes down to that. What have I been called to do and to be by the will of God concerning my personhood? And as I consider that, is there anything sufficiently compelling or constraining or alluring—anything that would constitute "the pleasures of sin"—that might pressure me or entice me to fall short of my God-given calling and settle for less than my own sincere individuality? Or am I willing even to "be mistreated"—that is, to suffer the threat or the conflict or the loss that might accompany my principle-based action of obeying what God has directed me to think and do? The answers to those questions will decide the integrity of my own personal commitment to truly being and becoming.

Some words of Jesus in the New Testament serve to bring this idea into even clearer focus. In an invitation to the most meaningful of all lives, where one's truest individuality will be safeguarded and expressed, Jesus declares in some of the best known words in the Gospel:

> Come to Me, all you who are weary and burdened, and I will give you rest. Take My yoke upon you, and learn from Me; for I am gentle and humble in heart, and you will find rest for your souls. For My yoke is easy, and My burden is light (Matthew 11:28-30).

In that wonderful declaration there is paradoxically indicated the place of greatest freedom and attainment possible in simply being and expressing one's own individual identity and person. It is found, amazingly enough and ironically enough in *conforming!*—in bearing *a yoke* and *submitting to a direction!* But this is no self-diminishing and self-negating kind of association into which we are invited. It is one that is life-enhancing and life-fulfilling in the extreme. And it is the final answer to where my uniqueness in the eyes of God and my role in the purposes of God are to be affirmed and empowered. That is the final rationale for how and why it must be that, in my quest for the full and profound life that I seek, yoked in living fellowship with Christ, all I have to do is be *unconventional.*

Chapter 22
All You Have To Do Is Be
VOLUNTARY

In the Upper Room, on the night before His death, Jesus shared with His disciples a most powerful and dramatic lesson in willing and unprompted service. As the twelve closest followers of the Lord sat at the table sharing in what was to be the Last Supper, we are told:

> (Jesus) got up from the meal, took off His outer clothing, and wrapped a towel around His waist. After that, He poured water into a basin and began to wash His disciples' feet, drying them with the towel that was wrapped around Him. When He had finished washing their feet, He put on His clothes, and returned to His place. "Do you understand what I have done for you?" He asked them. "You call Me 'Teacher' and 'Lord,' and rightly so, for that is what I am. Now that I, your Lord and Teacher, have washed your feet, you also should wash one another's feet. I have set you an example, that you should do as I have done for you." (John 13:4-5, 12-13).

"I have set you an example."
How do we, then, follow the example of "the Great Volunteer"?

A Voluntary Person Recognizes That Things Need To Be Done

It may be possible for me to earn a living by doing no more and no less than what is legally required of me. Maybe I can get a job where I can punch the time-clock at precisely the starting time in the morning and again at precisely the quitting time eight hours later. And maybe even within my eight hours of work I can very carefully stick to exactly what my job description requires of me, making sure that I do only what I am absolutely contractually bound to do, operating with cold and definitive precision. I guess, if that were the case, I could make a living in such a way. And, I am sure, I would at the same time be quite miserable. I would find such a situation sheer drudgery. I would probably end up counting the minutes and seconds to closing time finding that I was giving literally nothing to my job and that it was giving nothing back to me. But I guess I could do all that, and make a living at such a job in such a way.

Now, further, consider the above in the light of, not simply an occupation within which I earn a living, but an ongoing existence within which I forge an entire life. Suppose that I approach the whole matter of my personal expression in the total process of living—all my interactions in the give and take of the various involvements in which I share—in the same minimal way in which I could approach the prescriptions of my job. I could do all the things that a good citizen is legally required to do; and I wouldn't have to do any of the things that fall outside the definition of statutory obligation. I wouldn't have to concern myself about anything in the realms of compassion or graciousness or helpfulness. After all, there are government departments and social agencies and community programs—all funded by *my* taxes, I might add—that can provide a recourse for any person needing attention or help of any kind. In essence, I would say that the model to which I aspire is that of Ebenezer Scrooge who functioned just fine, thank you, before he had those visits from those interfering do-gooder Christmas Spirits! Yes, I suppose I could carry out my affairs and live my life in such an insulated and selfish way. But what kind of a life would it be? Would it be deep and sweet and fulfilling and vigorously challenging and satisfying? Would it reflect the joy and the thrill of mutual engagement with other persons? Or would it be narrow and rigid and sour and graspingly shallow and unfulfilling? Everything about my nature tells me that it would be the latter. And that is because, as an elemental part of a life that is vital and vibrant and expansive and enriched, I have to learn to give, and to do more than the bare minimum that the law demands; I have to learn to be *voluntary.* I need to learn the lesson of deliberate, freely-offered action that is done just because I can see that it needs to be done, and I am ready to do it. An old North American Indian legend gives some indication of why this is so.

> At the first, it is said, the all-powerful Earth-Namer took some red soil and formed man out of it. Just before man was completed, the Earth-Namer paused, and said, "Man has now been formed, except for his hands. What sort of hands shall I give him?"
>
> "Give him hands like mine," said the tortoise—"fins, so that he can swim easily in water."

> "No," said the coyote; "give him hands like mine—paws, so that he can run like the wind on land."
>
> All the animals clamored to have mankind be given hands like theirs, whether fins or paws or talons or claws; but the Earth-Namer simply smiled wisely, and then spoke.
>
> "No," He said: "I know what I will do. I will give man hands like mine—and then those good things which need doing on earth can be done by him, just as though they were done by me."

It is a picturesque story, but it carries a real and valid truth. We were not created in order that we might be guilty of the sin of caring only for or about ourselves. We were created in order that we might carry on the work of God by being voluntary and simply doing the things that need to be done.

A Voluntary Person Does Things FOR Persons— Not TO Them Or AT Them

Centuries ago, the Roman poet and philosopher Horace said something that has come down over the years as a wise and pertinent observation: "Who helps a man against his will does the same as murder him." This is truly so when the person who volunteers to provide some benefit or other to a chosen recipient—or *victim!*—does so out of a spirit of "laying on" whatever help is proffered, without due consideration of the appropriateness or necessity or even desirability of his or her actions. The unfortunate one who is at the receiving end of an insensitive contribution by some eager-beaver volunteer not only may not benefit, but may actually have his or her situation worsened through the burden of what is not so much given to as thrust upon him or her. We need to preface any volunteering with the simple but pertinent question, "Whose need is being met hereby, and whose agenda is being followed?"

Some volunteering really meets the criteria of misdirected aid-giving to the extent that it actually becomes a reverse explication of one very important biblical declaration. In Acts 20:35 Paul makes reference to the words the Lord Jesus Himself said: "It is more blessed to give than to receive." Yes, it is more blessed to give than to receive; but not in the way some volunteering of help or direction or money or assistance is given. Some volunteering is given from the vantage point of a superior assisting an inferior, and its greatest "blessing" is in the ego-boosting that the giver enjoys as a result. Consequently, the one receiving what is given is more abased than enriched, more humiliated than helped, more put down than lifted up by the whole transaction.

One is justified in being both suspicious and critical, and even resentful, of much avid volunteering of a self-serving sort; much as the young boy whom I once saw pictured in a certain cartoon, who was suspicious of the motives behind a certain action impinging on him. In the scene that is set out, a beleaguered-looking youngster is sitting at the table staring rather morosely and unappreciatively at the food that has been set before him. Turning to his mother he asks somewhat skeptically, "How come I'm the only kid on the block celebrating National Broccoli Week?" It's a good question; and to it the boy's mother would have what she would undoubtedly consider to be a good answer: "Because, even if you don't know it and appreciate it, broccoli is good for you; and even if I have to use subterfuge to get you to eat it, I will try to do what I think is best for you." Well, there may be some latitude for a concerned mother to use ingenious and unusual means in order to ensure a healthy diet for a dependent child—although, I really think "National Broccoli Week" is carrying even that a little too far! But in any event, that sort of attitude does not carry over very well into our relationships with one another. And I have to be careful in any volunteering that I do that I am not secretly trying to impose on you what would make *me* feel good in a given situation. We need to remember the dignity and the right to self-determination of every person. Apropos of which, I relate the following.

I still remember with regret something that happened a number of years ago in my own experience when I did an unintentional disservice to a family I was trying to help. This came about just before Christmas one year, during the season of peace on earth and goodwill to men; and it stemmed from what could only be called the best of motives expressed by the congregation of the church of which I was the minister at that time. The church I served had a very commendable practice of setting aside a special offering each month for what was known as the Benevolent Fund, with the purpose of that fund being to provide assistance to persons in various situations of need. The fund functioned totally at the discretion of the minister, so that any person who was helped could receive aid quite anonymously, assured that only the minister and the recipient would know where the money was going. That made for a setting where there was a minimum of embarrassment for anyone seeking help—no committee to go through, no need for a flock of people to know that one was receiving "charity." Moreover, because of the confidentiality of my pastoral role, I was often able to be the one to initiate the giving and receiving of help, making it unnecessary for persons to come and ask for help—something that most people find it very hard, and, sadly, also very demeaning to do. Thus, the church was able to volunteer help to many who genuinely needed it. And that brings me to the occasion to which I referred above, the occasion that I regret, as it occurred during one Christmas season.

Each year, in December, it was my custom to carry around with me a bunch of Christmas gift certificates purchased at a local supermarket. These were made out in varying dollar amounts, and it was my practice to dispense these discreetly in the form of ostensibly supplying a turkey for the festive season. A family would be given a certificate or certificates in the understanding that they could redeem them at the supermarket for the bird of their choice. Of course, they didn't need to buy a turkey at all if that was their preference; and the amount given was always more than the cost of even the biggest gobbler, so that there was a margin of additional help available to the recipients. This system seemed to work well, allowing for an exchange of season's greetings that was both natural and acceptable—except in the one case that I recall. I remember visiting in one home where uncertain employment and family health concerns were apparently putting a severe strain on the family budget and making it difficult for the parents to cope with the normal demands of living, let alone any seasonal extras. In that setting I tried as graciously and as naturally as I could to offer the customary "turkey" to the young mother to whom I was speaking. Unfortunately, she construed my words as a measure of insult, apparently in the perception that I must have thought them somehow inferior, to be offering them charity. She politely but coolly refused my offer. Moreover, in the days and months that followed, her attitude became increasingly one of withdrawal from the fellowship of the church; and I was certain that that was because she had felt demeaned by what she saw as my insensitive and heavy-handed do-goodism. My mistake was honest, and I wished immediately that I could have undone it. But I had done more harm than good because I had obviously not been sensitive enough to the dignity and self-esteem of the recipient of my action. I was too anxious to volunteer, and not sufficiently concerned with the personal feelings of the one I wanted to help. We need to base our voluntary action on *empathy*, avoiding the sin of *apathy*, but not falling into the trap of mere *sympathy*.

To be guilty of apathy is to commit the sin of being centered on ourselves. On the other hand, to let ourselves be caught up in mere sympathy is to lose our objectivity to the point where sentimentalism rather than strong compassion governs our response. Thus, we need to seek for a degree of sensitivity which allows us to feel what another is feeling and yet remain sufficiently distanced from the situation to be able to bring help, and not mere commiseration, to what is happening. Our response in any situation where there is need and where we can give of our selves or our resources in some way in order to help must avoid the extremes of tearful hand-wringing at one end of the spectrum—that only serves to get us and the person we blubber over wet—and the callous indifference of simply not caring, as long as we ourselves are not threatened, hurt, or inconvenienced.

A Voluntary Person Is Someone In The Flow Of Life

In the final analysis, a voluntary person is one who finds his or her own personhood enhanced by the things and deeds he or she offers—not in the sense of Little Jack Horner, with a self-congratulatory attitude of "What a good boy am I!" but in the manner of the Good Samaritan whose reward was the well-being of another person. It would seem to be a simple law of *being* and *becoming* that our own wholeness is part and parcel with the wholeness of other persons. Deny or ignore the need and the right of someone else to attain the fullest measure of character and individuality, and your own development as a vital and fulfilled human being will thereby be accordingly diminished and impoverished.

Elizabeth O'Connor narrates something relevant to this matter in her book, *Letters To Scattered Pilgrims*, in a chapter entitled "On Our Moving Center." I believe that center to which O'Connor refers—the place where we know ourselves as growing, seeking persons—is truly a dynamic, rather than a static, thing; and that we always will be striving after, and in pursuit of, the experience of *becoming* that must ultimately define us. And I believe our readiness to volunteer ourselves in the service of others is a vital factor in our progress towards personhood. O'Connor writes as follows:

> Recently, Janelle Goetcheus, a member of the Church of the Savior, wanted to bring into being a city health center with a number of medical and counseling services. Janelle is a medical doctor, who with her husband and children moved to the Washington area so that she might nurture her vision of working with the poor. The more she moved out on her vision, the more it unfolded until she reached a time of readiness in her spirit and issued her own call for the creation of structures that would have the potential of bringing a whole new quality of health care to inner city residents. She had no sooner announced her commitment to the vision than people essential to the new ministry came to join with her. One was Karen Michaelson, who, quite independently, had developed her concept of

> a ministry to the total person. The other was Chas Griffin, a therapist and old friend who was living in Buffalo, New York. Though he had an extensive practice, he was aware of feelings of envy when his friend shared with him what she as doing in Washington. When she called with the news of the health center, it was like a gong sounding the time in him. "I am coming," he said.[1]

What a beautiful expression!—"It was like a gong sounding the time in him." That gong, or something resembling it in its quality of summons or invitation, is what needs to sound and be heard in each one of us in our act of volunteering. It is a gong that tells us that now is the time for us to give or go or serve; and it is a sound that we ignore at the peril of falling short of our calling to personhood. How sad to turn an unheeding ear to that gong, or, worse, to just be so deaf that we don't even hear it! We need to be in the flow of who and what we are, in order to be ready to go with that flow in the spending of our selves and our resources in a cause larger than ourselves, as we truly move on towards *being* and *becoming* by being *voluntary*.

Notes

1 Elizabeth O'Connor, *Letters to Scattered Pilgrims* (New York: Harper and Row, 1979) p.114.

Chapter 23
All You Have To Do Is Be
WONDERING

Pussycat, Pussycat, where have you been?
"I've been to London to visit the Queen."
Pussycat, Pussycat, what did you do there?
"I frightened a little mouse under a chair."

Do you get the feeling that the Pussycat mentioned above had a less than perceptive sense of the occasion of his visit to London? Imagine all the beauty and impressiveness of that great capital city, with its magnificent architecture, towering and ornate! Imagine the sense of history and romance in the fabled place names there! And then imagine being ushered into the grand palace itself to "visit the Queen," with all the attendant pomp and ceremony to go along with that! And what is the most memorable and striking aspect of the cat's involvement in all that there was to see and to share in, in what most people would regard as a "once in a lifetime" experience? *"I frightened a little mouse under a chair!"*

The nursery rhyme is a parable, pointing to the blinkered way in which, all too often, we can perceive and respond to everything going on in our lives around us. Sadly, we are all too often deaf, dumb and blind to the rich and fulfilling possibilities of thrill and astonishment that life affords; and as a consequence we find our experience of life to be lamentably poorer and thinner and shallower than it can be and should be. Seldom, it seems, are we stirred by the sense that we have seen, or experienced or been caught up by something to shout about, something to write home about, something to *stop the presses* for! I think we need to put some *wonder* into our lives.

Wonder At THE WORLD YOU LIVE IN

> My God, I thank Thee who hast made
> The earth so bright;
> So full of splendor and of joy,
> Beauty and light;
> So many glorious things are here,
> Noble and right.[1]

When we have lost the capacity to wonder, or when that capacity is stunted and diminished, everything just seems dull and flat. We move about, experiencing and perceiving life at a minimally aesthetic level, blind and deaf and insensitive to the rich texture of our world. An old childhood rhyme and some contemporary facts related to it will perhaps point this up.

For many years now, children have been chanting a particular verse during their play, often in connection with skipping rope or playing hopscotch. It is a verse that sets out a compendium of possible occupations or callings that anyone might pursue in life. The most common version of that rhyme goes something like:

> A tinker, a tailor, a cowboy, a sailor;
> Rich man, poor man, beggar-man, thief,
> A doctor, a lawyer, a merchant chief.

I count eleven possibilities within those lines; eleven categories within which the mind of a child would see whatever possibilities of engagement and involvement might lie before any individual. Now, of course, nobody ever said that the scope of that verse was exhaustive or all-inclusive; but for many years it has been understood to be at least comprehensive; and generally speaking, generations of children have sung those words and have been at least reasonably satisfied that they have covered at least most of the bases. But I wonder if anybody could sing those words today and feel that they really made any sense, in view of the following piece of information.

In 2005, the United States Government issued a two-volume, 1300-page *Dictionary of Occupational Titles,* an enlarged update of previously published volumes, detailing tasks performed, educational requirements and skills needed for more than *twelve thousand* types of jobs. That number is not a misprint. Those job categories all exist for anyone to consider; prompting two comments. One: it would be rather difficult, would it not, for any boy or girl to skip to a recitation of that mammoth list of possibilities! And two: it rather wants to make you be careful, doesn't it, the next time you're tempted to ask a child, "What do you want to be when you grow up?"!

I mention this statistic simply to make an emphasis by comparison. If it is possible that a child could naively chant out a compendium of eleven different job options, and believe that he or she was thus encompassing the entire field of possible vocational choices—with, meanwhile, over twelve thousand identified occupations looming in the background—so it is possible, and so, I am convinced, it is often the case, that a melancholy, myopic individual can slouch disconsolately through life convinced that there is hardly anything of sheer marvel or pure delight to be seen and experienced—all the while surrounded and overarched and virtually besieged on every hand by the most incredible realities to be virtually gasped at, and thrilled at, and experienced with amazement and joy.

> Earth's crammed with heaven,
> And every common bush aflame with God;
> But only he who sees takes of his shoes;
> The rest sit 'round and pluck blackberries.[2]

Wonder at YOURSELF

It's marvelous enough that the world around us is so beautiful and enchanting. It's even more breathtaking that we are who and what we are as persons. "I am fearfully and wonderfully made!" the Psalmist declared (Psalm 139:14). In the light of which Shakespeare has Hamlet declare in one place in wonder and eager joy,

> What a piece of work is man! How noble in reason! How infinite in faculty! In form and moving how express and admirable! In action how like an angel! In apprehension how like a god! The beauty of the world! The paragon of animals![3]

Now, as the saying goes, if we could only live up to those press clippings! And the marvelous thing is that we can!—in at least three wonderful ways.

1. Expansiveness

Frequently, in the *Book of Psalms,* there is employed an interesting figure of speech to refer to the kind of life that the writer there longs to live to some measure of fullness, as he expresses a desire for growth towards *becoming.* Over and over again we read exclamations addressed to God in terms like "The Lord brought me out into a spacious place," or "You broaden the path beneath me"(Psalm 18:18-19, 36). Such statements have nothing to do with literal, physical settings; they are references to spiritual, emotional and psychological realities. They speak of life virtually opening up before us with the great potential for freedom, growth and expansion that is ours for the knowing.

2. Enrichment

Life is an experience of growth in *becoming* as we are enhanced as persons in and through everything that we meet. We not only confront and are confronted by life; we draw sustenance and nourishment from our engagement with it. Our minds, spirits and wills are strengthened and promoted through our daily living and—to quote a good biblical notion—we find that we literally "go from strength to strength"(Psalm 84:7). Let me indicate how this may be so by making reference to what is without doubt the most crushing and overwhelming experience that it is possible for any of us to undergo—the experience of bereavement. We may suffer many losses. We may undergo all kinds of hardships and trials. We may lose our money, our job, and even our health. We may be slandered and maligned. We may be cheated and deceived. Yet, even in the face of the "many dangers, toils and snares" that we are called on to face and go through, somehow we seem to be able to call up hidden resources from within the human spirit to not only address those things and make our way through them, but to actually draw strength from our experiences so that we are deeper and hardier and even purer and better persons for having borne the difficulty and the pain.

But bereavement takes all that kind of perception to its ultimate point of testing. It's one thing to suffer the loss of goods, reputation, position or health. We can still rise again from the dust and ashes of humiliation and loss, to go on anew. But when death—sometimes cruelly and callously, sometimes mockingly and mercilessly—robs us of someone whom we have held more dear than life itself, and we are left with the aching emptiness and the inconsolable grief that accompanies that; doesn't that negate the whole notion of being able to grow and deepen as persons through our trial? Well, in this regard consider two expressions associated with the occasion of death, both expressions being taken from the liturgy for *The Burial of the Dead.*

First, a line of rather desolate acknowledgement from a prayer of obedience—the phrase, "the changes of life leave us poorer and sadder." Sometimes we think that that is all they can do. Sometimes we think, in our broken-heartedness, that we can find no grace in what has come into our lives, simply because of what has been taken out of our lives. We will always be "poorer and sadder" because of our loss. We may well carry the scar of this experience with us for the rest of our lives.

But also consider this: a line from yet another prayer, this one a prayer of faith and trust: "May this visitation of death in our midst be seen in the light of Your love and goodness. May it minister to a truer and holier life in our souls." What a daring and even presumptuous petition that is! Can a visitation of death actually minister to us in such a way that even this experience can be turned to our personal deepening and growth? Well, let me ask: if it can't, and if it isn't, then what is the ultimate outcome of it to be? Shall the memory that we hold and the love that we cherish be turned against our very selves in bitterness and cynicism? How does that honor the one whom we have lost? Rather, is it not more fitting that the tender and profound love that has endeared the lost one to us should continue to contribute to our experience of him or her as we go on to love that person in a new way that allows the one who has died to move on to the new experience that awaits him or her even as we go on to the new phase of life that lies before us? Such questioning is not meant to be merely speculative. It points to something solidly experiential. I do not speak thus glibly. In my capacity as a minister I have read both of the lines I have quoted above from the Church's prayers many, many times as I have shared with many, many persons in their experience of mourning; and I have also, personally and painfully, heard those lines read by other officiating clergy as I have, myself, sat in the seat of those who mourn. I write as I do only because I truly believe in the God-given capacity of the human spirit to grow in the process of becoming a deeper and better person in and through every experience that can come in life or death.

3. Potentiality

Then, consider the third facet which arises out of the attitude of wondering at yourself, which is the innate and unquenchable characteristic of possibility that is at the heart of our human nature. Some words of promise from Isaiah give a powerful indication of what I mean.

> Forget the former things; do not dwell on the past. See, I am doing a new thing! Now it springs up; do you not perceive it? (Isaiah 43:18).

The instruction God gives to His people there does not encourage us simply to try to forget all about the past, to try to block it out of our memories as though it never happened. That would be inadvisable even if it were possible. In many instances it would also be ungrateful. No, what is urged in Isaiah's exhortation is that we do not *dwell* on that which is past, that we do not keep either harking back to joys that are gone or reminding ourselves of sorrow, sin, or failure with which we continue to berate or negate ourselves. Don't "remember" the past to the place where it fills the whole screen of your thinking. Don't "consider" it by letting it dictate your mind-set or your level of anticipation. Don't act as though you thought that the past was the only viable paradigm and chart of possibilities for the future. The glorious reality that God affirms for us is that the future is always one of openness and potential. Bear that in mind, and you will be led to a joyful attitude of wonder at what you are designed and destined for as the will and purpose of God for your *becoming* unfold more and more before you every day.

Wonder At GOD

Of all the facts of our existence, of all the great matters upon which we might reflect in wondering awe, the one supreme reality that stands out above everything else is the person and nature of God as revealed in His creation of us and His care for us.

"To whom, then, will you compare God? What image will you compare Him to?" the prophet asks rhetorically (Isaiah 40:18). No comparison can be made; because God, in eternal greatness and grandeur, is like no other. There is no other like Him in holiness, in might, in glory, in utter perfection. He is the completely effulgent and ineffable one—"the blessed and only Ruler, the King of Kings and Lord of Lords who alone is immortal and who lives in unapproachable light, whom no one has seen or can see" (1 Timothy 6:15-16). Before the awesome presence of such a one it is our part to bow in humility and reverence and wondering awe. And yet this God is the one who graciously comes to us and touches our lives with the goodness and the glory of His person and His actions.

Consider one biblical expression that can shed some light on this notion, as this expression is rendered in two different translations. First, the customary rendering of this verse: "Who can proclaim the mighty acts of the Lord?" (Psalm 106:2KJV). What does that question connote? Well, for me, when I read that, my mind jumps to a natural understanding of the key words, "mighty acts;" and I see those acts as being marvelous expressions of divine power and purpose—deeds of unparalleled authority, impressive in their grand and sovereign character—"Stand back, and see the mighty things that God can do, and *does!*" Our God is a God of might and sovereign power.

But consider another version of those same words, this one from The Psalter in *the Book of Common Prayer.* There, Psalm 106:2 is set forth as follows: "Who can express the *noble* acts of the Lord?"(emphasis added.) And to my mind, the difference in import is significant. God's deeds are not just mighty and impressive, as marvelous as that might be. They are *noble,* as comforting and reassuring as that is. They are acts of integrity, of good and right purpose, admirable in their intent and beneficent in their result. They are the good and caring actions of a Lord "whose compassions never fail," who "does not willingly bring affliction or grief on anyone," but who "will show compassion, so great is His unfailing love" ((Lamentations 3:32-33). Those words engender a great sense of trust and confidence in God. I embrace not just His power, but His compassion and trustworthiness; and I can commend myself in certainty to the love and care of His will being worked out in my life. And I think this is something that is of immensely practical importance and application. Too often, I think, we are guilty of suspecting that God sometimes acts in our lives with less than truly noble—or at least with less than *apparently* noble—motives and intentions. And that makes me think of a possible reaction that we might offer to such a perception. We have an expression that is used in our society that refers to the practice of impugning or maligning the intentions or purposes of any person. We speak, in those circumstances, of the tendency to "bad-mouth" the individual under consideration. Well, it may sound too extreme to say that on occasion we might actually go so far as to "bad-mouth" God—(essentially what I think the Bible means when it speaks of "murmuring against" Him; *i.e.,* grousing or carping about God behind His back—cf. Exodus 16:7,8,9 KJV). But even if we don't go so far as to be guilty of "bad-mouthing" God, I nonetheless think that it is the case more commonly than we might wish to acknowledge that we do at least bad-*think* Him. And I believe that to a large extent that is the case because we have failed to perceive that His actions towards us—even though they may not be immediately obvious as being so—are truly *noble;* because He is—truly, He cannot be other than—compassionate and trustworthy. He is loving and merciful; and He cannot and will not act in any way towards us that is not in keeping with his caring and saving nature.

That being the case, let us learn to feed our souls and enrich our minds on the wonder of *wonder.*

Notes

[1] Adelaide A. Procter, 1825-1864, from her hymn, "My God, I thank Thee," 1858.

[2] Elizabeth Barrett Browning, 1806-1861, "Aurora Leigh #38, Book VII

[3] William Shakespeare, 1564-1616, *Hamlet,* Act II, Scene 2.

Chapter 24
All You Have To Do Is Be
XENOPHILIC

This part of our consideration is actually an extended exercise wherein we seek to accentuate the positive in a hope that we may truly eliminate the negative. "Xenophobia" is a word that has come over into English from the Greek, and is in common and accepted use. It is made up of two Greek roots: the word *xenos,* meaning "stranger," or "alien;" and the word *phobos,* meaning "fear." Thus, it means, very simply, fear of, or aversion towards, anything or anyone that is strange or foreign.

A much less familiar term is the word "xenophilia"—a word that presents the opposite concept to that of fearing or hating what is different from us. It begins with the same root word, *xenos,* to denote "stranger," or "alien;" but couples it with the Greek term *phileo,* which means "love." Thus to be xenophilic is to be open to, and receptive of, and grounded in love towards, other persons—in particular, persons unlike us or unfamiliar to us.

So, the thrust of this chapter of our consideration is: Out with the xenophobic, and in with the xenophilic!

Being Xenophilic Overcomes Suspicion And Mistrust

"Birds of a feather flock together." So goes the old adage, revealing something profound about more than our avian friends. It appears to be a deep-seated reality within the makeup of human beings that *persons* who have similar backgrounds or convictions or values also tend to "flock together" while having little to do with those who are simply recognized or categorized as being "different." And we have terms that we use to define and express the less than cordial attitudes that are often generated and displayed in such circumstances. We speak of "outsiders," and "foreigners"—words that automatically break society down into divisions of "us" and "them." And we may even sharpen the lines of distinction by using a deliberately negative and derogatory term such as "barbarian" to refer to someone who is really beyond the pale. In any event, what we are referring to is essentially those with whom we feel we have little in common and with whom we want little to do. And they don't have to be "classic" in nature for me to feel that way about them, either. That is, persons for whom I feel little affinity and less affection do not need to be from another planet or from another country in order for me to regard them as being "aliens" and "foreigners." And they don't have to come from some savage, untamed, recently discovered part of the world for me to consider them as uncouth and unrefined barbarians. Rather, they really only need to be "other," and I can take it from there. That's a serious situation, and one that hampers any free and generous relating to other persons on my part. It is truly something that needs to be set right. So, what's to be done? Well, let's think first about several things that are *not* to be done, several attitudes of response to other persons that are *not* to be expressed.

1. Condescension

Surely there are few things more demeaning and irritating than the perception that one is being patronized. Whether it is based on the attitude of "holier than thou," or "richer than thou," or "more learned than thou," or "more refined than thou," or just plain, all-around "better than thou," the final import is always the same: "I'm only talking with you, or dealing with you, or having anything at all to do with you because I am so nice and you are so needy." Someone once observed, "A truly gracious personality is like a public banquet to which everyone is invited." By comparison, who can feel very thrilled with the meager crumbs which are dispensed by a condescending person who acts only from a position of arrogance and disdain?

2. Bogus Affirmation and Deliberate Manipulation

Today we live in a world where it is considered a tremendous asset to be able to adroitly handle and deal with people—to have, as our jargon puts it, "people smarts." Whether it's in the area of selling something, or getting someone to agree to something, or settling some difference or dispute between persons, that individual who can moderate by spreading oil on the waters, or motivate by lighting a fire under someone, or simply arbitrate by making everyone involved think that they got the best of the deal, is much in demand and highly esteemed. It's all in knowing what strings to pull, what buttons to push, what levers to yank. A few positive strokes here, some behavior modification there, a little ego-boosting all around; and everybody's happy. Well, please be aware that I have deliberately made that description a caricature. It's not affirmation or positive strokes or motivation or arbitration in themselves that are suspect. Those can all be legitimate and genuinely helpful factors when they are brought sincerely into play. But those things can also be wrong when they are basically phony, when they spring from an attitude that is less than genuinely *xenophilic.* "In the old days," a folk saying goes, "we loved people and used things. Now we use people and love things." We need to learn to get back on track again.

3. Live and Let Live

At first glance, this motto may seem to be a reasonable and even commendable way to deal with complex issues of varying and even contrary ways of believing, thinking and acting. "You go your way, and I'll go mine," it seems to be saying; which has a ring of generosity and permission about it that makes it sound attractive—as long as we gloss over the unfortunate, negating proviso which seems logically to follow, namely, *"and never the twain shall meet!"* That may be marginally better than outright condescension or manipulation, but it is still not a sufficient basis on which to relate to other persons in a mutually constructive and appreciative way; and it certainly does not reflect the attitude and practice of Jesus who went out of His way to mingle with and relate to all kinds and classes of people, whether any person might be a Pharisee, a Samaritan, an adulteress, a leper, a tax collector, or whatever or whoever. And in the picture of the Kingdom of Heaven at the end of the age that Jesus presented, everyone is invited to the great feast—the lame, the halt, the blind, the rich, the poor—and all are to be received and welcomed and loved. And at that final table, it should be stressed, there will be no preference of place given on the basis of the flimsy distinctions that we set so much store by now in our relationships with one another. No one then will be either above or below the salt. There will be no box seats and no bleachers. Every person will be as warmly received and as dearly cherished as all the others.

Being Xenophilic Is The Positive Element That Eliminates The Negative

A few years ago, on the first occasion of what was to become an annual event, a group of grammarians convened a symposium which made the news when those language specialists compiled and released to the public what they called *A Dishonor List Of Words To Be Banished Forever From The Queen's English.* Words on this contrapositive list were selected on the basis of misuse, mal-use and overuse, as well as being just generally of no use. They included such obvious expressions as "secluded privacy" and "free gift." "Cutting edge," as in the cutting edge of fashion or research, was also nominated for banishment on the premise that someone could get badly slashed working with such an expression. Another proscribed phrase was "on a roll," as in "That's his third touchdown tonight. He's on a roll." It was pointed out that being on a roll is fine for hamburgers, hot dogs and sesame seeds, but not people.

I find the above reference both interesting and amusing. I also find it both provocative and evocative, because it sets me to thinking of some other words that, hopefully, might also some day be banished from our language by the force of an awakened and noble-minded consensus. I refer to such words as narrow-mindedness, prejudice, racism, sexism, class-consciousness, bigotry and discrimination. Those words and the negative and destructive attitudes they connote could all be banished if only we ourselves were to become sufficiently aroused to see that they were! We could pack them all up and get rid of them forever if we were to take the one simple and resolute step of determining to live consistently in a spirit and manner of being *xenophilic.* And that calls for doing something more than merely hoping that that might happen. We need to seize and to build on the notion of being increasingly and intentionally inclusive in our caring for and sharing with others. Our concern ought to be that we are not distanced or insulated from any other person or persons by the fellowship-inhibiting, relationship-nullifying barriers that the differences between us make it so easy to erect. Our hearts ought to truly yearn for the privilege and the pleasure of affirming and sustaining one another in our universal search for the will of God and the experience of God. We need to pray for one another, care about one another, and help one another. And that "one another," according to Jesus, does not mean just those who think, believe, and act the way we do.

> You have heard that it was said, "love your neighbor and hate your enemy." But I tell you, love your enemies and pray for those who persecute you, that you may be sons of your Father in heaven. He causes His sun to rise on the evil and the good, and sends rain on the righteous and the unrighteous. If you love those who love you, what reward will you get? Are not even the tax collectors doing that? And if you greet only your brothers, what are you doing more than others? Do not even pagans do that? (Matthew 5:43-47).

Such a "royal law of love" surely goes about as far as it is possible to go with words in order to normalize the practice of acting in a truly *xenophilic* manner. And it challenges me to respond in a way that truly reflects my commitment to the principle of personal growth and becoming, particularly as my professed spirit of largeness and good will is stretched to include those who may disagree with or differ from me—to those, indeed, who may disagree with or differ from me very sharply and profoundly, even in areas that bear very crucially upon my very self-definition and identity. Can we apply the golden rule of Jesus not only hypothetically, in broadly philosophical terms, but pointedly and personally in the everyday things that make up life and loom so large in our considerations? I refer to those things which, unfortunately, frequently seem to become stumbling blocks to us—such things as racial origin, gender, educational attainment, cultural and religious diversity, political and philosophical ideology, and other items all the way from the words and music we use when we worship to the food we eat and the table manners we employ when we eat it. And, further, have I been so imbued with the spirit of my Lord that I can hold to the deepest sense of what is precious and even inviolable for me without impugning the right of someone else to hold, with equal tenacity, to principles that are not the same as mine? And can I do that gladly and respectfully and not merely grudgingly—with a sincere attitude of generosity, and not with a secret sense of resentment or distaste?

Being Xenophilic Gives Expression To The Explicit Will Of God

As someone once observed, the fabric of human existence is really something like a spider's web. Touch one part, no matter how remote its location, and the whole sensitive mesh responds. And tear one part, no matter how far it is from the rest, and the whole fragile network is weakened and placed in jeopardy. The fact is that, by the very nature of our being in this world, we are involved in a web of inter-meshing mutuality—a truth that is becoming more and more clear as time goes by and our "global village" becomes more and more a "global neighborhood," eventually, one may hope, to be recognized and affirmed as a "global family." And that last phrase is more than just a figure of speech. "From one man (God) made every nation that they should inhabit the whole earth," St. Paul affirmed in a sermon (Acts 17:26).

Startling thought, isn't it? We all spring from the same stock. Which means that, in fact, when we trace our genealogies and pedigrees back far enough, we are not really "alien" to one another at all. Rather—*surprise, surprise!*—we are all really long lost sisters and brothers to one another! That's why the ultimate purpose of our life together in this world, the ultimate goal towards which we strive, is not really the creation or establishment of any sort of any political or territorial—but essentially separated or distinctive—lowest common denominator co-existence, as significant or utilitarian as that sort of thing might or might not be; but the simple experience and expression and experience of a great big joyous and exhilarating family reunion!

Norman Vincent Peale adds a homely but relevant illustration concerning how this fact, then, relates and inter-relates us.

> I once heard a lecture in which the speaker talked about the great redwood trees of California, those magnificent giants of the forest towering as much as three hundred feet in the air. "You'd think that such tall trees would require very deep roots," the speaker said. "Actually, redwoods have a very shallow root system, designed to capture all the surface moisture possible. These roots spread out in all directions, and as a result, all the roots of all the trees in a redwood grove are intertwined. They are locked together so that when the wind blows or a storm strikes, all the trees support and sustain one another. That is why you almost never see a redwood standing alone. They need one another to survive.[1]

That's the way we, as persons, were designed by God; and life really will not work as it should work any other way. To disavow my inter-relatedness with every other human being, and to deny that my attainment of full personhood and happiness is inextricably involved with their freedom and right to *be* and to *become*, is to fail to grasp the divine plan for us all and to short-circuit the divine intent. The self-respect and the sense of personal worth that allow us confidently to pursue the great goal of our fullest personhood will only truly be ours as we actively wish and assert the same blessing for all other human beings. In a word, in our quest for the most profound experience of *being* and *becoming*, all we have to do is be *xenophilic*.

Notes

1 Norman Vincent Peale, *Imaging* (Carmel, New York: Guideposts, 1982. Used with special arrangement with Fleming H. Revell Company) p.78.

Chapter 25
All You Have To Do Is Be
YOUTHFUL

To be deliberately *youthful* as a part of our quest for fullest personhood is not a chronologically based thing, having to do with the amount of time that has elapsed since the day of our birth. Rather, it is a matter of being youthful in essence, in the very way one sees and addresses life; possessed always of the qualities of freshness and anticipation and *élan vital;* rejoicing in an innate, ever-unfolding capacity for development and a never-ending potential for discovery and growth. Such a wonderful quality of inner youngness need never fade. In fact, it really ought to be possible to retain and refine the essence of personal freshness as one grows older and more experienced in the way of true *becoming*.

Being Youthful Involves The Matter Of PERSPECTIVE

Perhaps a comparison of two particular characters may allow us to grasp the import of this notion. Consider, on the one hand, the man, Ned Ludd, a person of dubious distinction, concerning whom history has recorded only one action—and that a mark of infamy; and, on the other hand, the mythical Greek hero, Ulysses, whose exploits are truly legend.

Ned Ludd is said to have run amuck and smashed some of the shop furnishings of an early manufacturer in Leicestershire, England, back in 1779, in the belief that the introduction and use of mechanized equipment was not *progress,* but an unwelcome and upsetting intrusion of unnatural processes into the very way of life of ordinary people. Ned preferred the old way of doing things, and felt threatened in the extreme by the new and the unknown. That's really about all we know of him, and yet it is enough to ensure that both he and his world-view live on. You see, that action of Ned Ludd's was later recalled and a descriptive term coined from it when, some years afterwards, in 1811, an organized band of workers went on a rampage in the English Midlands, smashing and destroying industrial machinery because they saw it as an invasive and destructive force in the world. Mechanization was deemed contrary to the natural order of things. If anything was to be made for consumption and use within society, it was asserted, it should be done in the time-honored way of being made by human hands. People should not be made redundant by impersonal machines, and the impassioned resisters of the insidious tide of change became rioters in order to make their point. Those who espoused and enshrined the past and acted accordingly in a determinedly reactionary way, being unable to see any possibility for growth and development in the unfolding future, were called simply, "Luddites." And if I were to conjecture any sort of a symbol to represent their attitude and their mind-set, I could think of nothing more appropriate than a straitjacket.

Ulysses, on the other end of the spectrum, represents a person who just never stopped seeing the openness of life as it lay before him. Even at an advanced age, after a life full of wanderings and exploits, he was further pulled irresistibly forward by the call of adventure, to set forth to discover what he had never known, to sail to where he had never been, and to undertake things that he had never done: "To strive, to seek, to find, and not to yield," as Tennyson describes it.[1] And our language has incorporated a term based on his actions, as well, the adjective, "Ulyssean;" which is a word used to describe someone who refuses to stagnate within life but who continually rises to new opportunities and seizes new challenges to learn and discover and create and become. And if I were to try to represent that sort of person by a symbol, in this case the thing that comes immediately to mind is a pair of wings.

Often, we associate the tragedy of being emotionally "old" with the process of physical aging, as though it were a given truth that the older you get the more likely you are to be a "stick-in-the-mud." But it is just as possible, unfortunately, to be shortsighted and pessimistic when one is quite young as when one is pronouncedly old. Age has no monopoly on the bent for being bearish, on the penchant for living in the pits. It is perspective that makes the difference, and we are all responsible for our perspective, no matter how old or young we may be. Apropos of which, consider the following dialogue.

The Pleistocene Gap

He came wandering into the cave out of the Pleistocene mist, idly scraping the bark off a twig with a sharpened stone.

"Where have you been?" asked his mother, giving the rabbit on the spit another turn over the fire.

"Outside."

"Where outside?"

"Just outside."

"Doing what?" she persisted.

"Just thinking. Sitting and thinking," he replied wearily. Then he sank onto the bearskin by the fire.

"You do too much thinking," she said, with an edge in her voice. "There are things that need to be done. We need new arrows and spear heads. Baskets need weaving. Your father is getting a little disgusted with your lack of help."

"Oh, Mom!" he said, flinging the twig into the fire, "What do you and Dad know? Don't you realize we have no future? Our race is doomed! What good is it going to do to make better spears and arrows when the game is disappearing? Why make new baskets when the berries are giving out?

"Don't you realize that it's just a matter of time? There are just too many of us for the food supply. Why, just the other day there were several fights over a single blackberry bush! And besides, with the invention of the bow and arrow, the whole race could be wiped out overnight. Things can't go on like this forever. There's just no way out. Nobody will limit his number of children. Each tribe is afraid the other will become larger and stronger and take over. We live with a sort of balance of terror. It's all so pointless. There's nothing to do. The council of elders just sit around the fire grunting and scratching their fleas. They won't listen to those of us who really know what's happening. We'll just have to resign ourselves to the end."

"Perhaps if you presented some alternative . . ." the mother began.

"There is no alternative!" he snapped.

"Well," the mother offered hesitantly, "perhaps there's no alternative in sight; but God could provide one. He might help us understand why some berry bushes grow larger than others, so that we could make them all grow big . . ."

"God!" he shouted. "You dream!" And still shaking his head, he rose and marched out into the mist.[2]

Eyes that are old and dull, spiritually and emotionally, focus with an outlook of pessimism on life. But a truly *youthful* perspective will allow any person to see life in terms of promise and hope. And it doesn't matter how many birthdays you've had. It really does all depend on how you look at it.

Being Youthful Involves The Matter Of PROSPECT

When you're truly young enough at the deepest center of your being, you revel in an attitude of possibility and envisionment. You deeply believe that there is no set of circumstances that you can possibly be brought into by any unfolding of events that does not contain the factors of hope and possibility. I saw something once in the window of our local transit authority that reminded me of the intrinsic quality of prospect that is at the heart of true personal youthfulness. One day I was walking along the sidewalk in front of the bus company's headquarters when my eye was caught by a large and colorful display that had been set up in the window. The display actually embodied an announcement that the transit commission wanted to bring to the attention of the public—a notice concerning the revamping of the major bus routes within the city and the outlying areas of the community. There were a number of rather sweeping and even radical changes in the offing, and I'm sure that the transit officials were well aware that those changes would be perceived by many bus patrons as negative moves. Long-time bus riders, particularly, might well feel lost in the turmoil and upheaval of changed routes and schedules. Truly, for many it could seem like the end of the normal and the imposition of the novel. So the transit authorities wanted to lessen the possibility of a negative reaction and a sense of disgruntlement on the part of their clientele and to set out the forthcoming changes in a more positive and appealing light. That's what the display in their window was all about. And for me, it worked. Though I was not a bus rider myself, I really felt that if I had been I would have been prepared to accept and even anticipate the forthcoming revision of services because the notice in the window managed to arouse in me a sense of prospect that was marked by both curiosity and hope. The notice in the window was comprised of a large map of the area served by various buses, on which were indicated in one color the old routes and in another color the new routes, with comments in boxes indicating how and why the new routes would better serve everyone involved. But what really impressed me and won me over was not the detailed outline of the upcoming changes, but the statement in big letters that ran across the top of the whole display. It was a clever and deliberate seizing of an all too common attitude and phrase associated with change and the dissolving of past patterns. It simply took the old pessimistic and doom-saying expression, "Be prepared: The End is Coming," and turned it around into an upbeat statement of anticipation and expectancy by boldly declaring for all to see, "Get Ready! The *Beginning* is Coming!" That sure sounded biblical to me! It sounded like what Jesus was constantly asserting. It seemed to be saying, "Don't spend your time moaning and lamenting. Believe that the way ahead is just that—a way *forward*, a way of prospect that is bright with openness and promise to all who approach it with a *youthful* spirit of trust and anticipation."

You Who Fear Change

You who fear change are like these sheep who turn
Back from cold mountain creeks, and drink
Only in small familiar pools, or suck
Green milk of these marshy ponds that lie
Round and unmoving in a valley's palm.

O slow and complacent muzzles, does it mean
Nothing to you that dust and drouth
Shrivel the little pools, and dung
Stains the warm stagnant water where the steers
Follow your little pathways to this pond?

Time fouls still water and slime lies
Mucous and soft above all ponds.
The lake by living springs unfed
Shrinks to a caking slough. Blind is that shepherd who would lead
his sheep
Back to these steer-trampled waters![3]

The Good Shepherd who leads us does not take us on a poor, pathetic retreat back to stagnant waters. He leads us "by streams where living waters flow," always towards *being* and *becoming.*

Being Youthful Involves The Matter Of PLAYFULNESS

By "playfulness" in our approach to life I do not mean a mere spirit of levity and a lack of seriousness—an attitude of flippancy and shallowness that simply says, "Laugh it off," no matter what the circumstances may be. Rather, I am proposing that we realize and exhibit in our lives an attitude that comes very naturally out of an appropriate grasp of perspective and a confident belief in prospect. If we enjoy the confidence that our God is graciously leading us, why should we march grimly through life with our brows furrowed, our muscles tightened, our fists clenched and our teeth gritted? Why should we not be free to taste and experience life with a buoyant joyfulness that will underlie everything that is a part of our life's adventure?

Many years ago, when I was in the middle grades of elementary school, I learned a lesson about the simple psychological validity of approaching life with a spirit of playfulness. Periodically, in those days, our teacher used to administer an arithmetic test, comprised of short problems of addition, subtraction, multiplication and division. Each pupil was issued a sheet on which an array of questions was set out, and was required to complete the work there. Actually, that presented no real difficulty for me. The problems were straightforward and were designed only to gauge the pupil's level of competence in the four arithmetical processes. Since I was quite skilled at that sort of thing, the solving of those assigned problems should have been very easy for me—and it would have been, too, except for one thing. There was a time limit imposed. As I remember, for some reason we were allowed precisely twelve minutes to complete the test. Then it was "Pencils down," and the work was collected. And that time limit was my undoing. I became so conscious of the need to get the work done within the allotted time-frame that I became nervous and apprehensive and spent more time glancing up at the clock and worrying that I wasn't going to make it than I did in actually working on the test. The outcome of that was that my test results were never better than mediocre, which puzzled the teacher because my daily work showed that I obviously could and should do better. And it wasn't until I learned to stop worrying about the clock and just go ahead and light-heartedly do the assignment as an exercise in fun that I finally managed to pull myself out of the trap that I had created for myself. Imagine! A nine-year-old kid having to be reminded of the importance of playfulness!

Urban T. Holmes shares the following "fairy tale."

The Girl With The Red Balloon

Once upon a time, in a little village by the sea, lived a little girl named Lucinda. They called her "that girl with the red balloon." Lucinda always carried a bright red balloon which was tied to a long silver string clutched tightly in her hand. Many of the people in the village laughed at Lucinda and her red balloon. Lucinda was just a little girl, however, and it was perfectly acceptable for small children to play with red balloons.

When she was very little, Lucinda tried to explain about her red balloon. For instance, the red balloon was good for leading her somewhere—to beautiful fields, to the ocean and its crashing waves, to a warm place where Lucinda felt love. But the balloon could also lead the little girl to dark, mysterious caves which frightened her, or sad forests of grief which made her cry, or into the midst of quarrels. Then she felt great anger; but it all went together.

The red balloon was also excellent for seeing. If she looked at her village, her friends, or the forest through the red balloon, she saw things that others did not see. In the beginning, Lucinda tried to tell others about what she saw. They laughed, and Lucinda learned not to explain about her red balloon.

Lucinda was as happy as could be expected, until one day somebody said, "Lucinda, you are too old for a red balloon. It was okay when you were a little child, but now you are almost a woman. You must let that stupid balloon go, and be mature." Lucinda held on tighter and tighter; but life became more and more difficult. One particularly difficult day the people were saying things like: "You are always over-dramatizing with that stupid red balloon in your hand," and ""if you let go of that ridiculous red balloon, you might accomplish something." Lucinda then made a decision. She knew she had to keep the red balloon; but she could hide it. The question was, Where? It had to be close to her, but it had to be well hidden. So she hid the balloon inside her head.

While this hiding place fitted the criteria for closeness and secrecy, it had its disadvantages. It gave her a terrible headache. It was very difficult, as well, to laugh and shake one's head with a red balloon stuffed inside. It was also difficult to cry, to be afraid, or even to get angry. There was a danger of the balloon popping out and being lost or discovered. To keep the balloon from doing this, Lucinda had to scrunch up her eyes, and seeing became very difficult. So, while the balloon was close, it was no longer useful for leading and seeing.

People did stop laughing, and they complimented Lucinda on her new adulthood. She got married and had babies. She even went to work in an important job in the village. Her headache got progressively worse, however, and she almost forgot about flowers,

> waves, warm places, caves, forests, and seeing things through red balloons.
>
> One day, while watching her children through scrunched-up eyes, she thought she saw something familiar in the hand of one of them. She tried and tried to see what it was, but she knew that if she was really to see it she would have to open wide her eyes. She knew what would happen if she did. But, being a good mother, and not wanting her child to have anything harmful, she did open her eyes. Just as she saw a red balloon on the end of a silver string in the hand of her child, she cried out—and out popped her own red balloon. It looked so beautiful, and it felt so good not to have that balloon in her head any more! She could see again, and everything appeared as new. So Lucinda decided to leave the balloon out in the open on a silver string. She laughed and laughed and laughed.
>
> Lucinda did not live happily ever after. People now laugh at her, and call her "spacey" and "childish," and tell her she has no common sense. The red balloon does not always lead Lucinda into beautiful fields of flowers. Dark caves are also there, as well as sad forests, and quarrels. When she looks through the red balloon, she does not always see beauty and happiness. But Lucinda did live *truly* ever after.[4]

"Winter is on my head," Victor Hugo wrote, when well on in years; "but eternal spring is in my heart." Maybe we should take as our final word for what lies ahead a paraphrase of a famous line by Robert Browning, and say: "Grow *young* with me! The best is yet to be."

Notes

1. Alfred Lord Tennyson, 1809-1892, Ulysses, 1842
2. "Eutychus V" from *Christianity Today,* January 7, 1972. Used by permission, Christianity Today, 1972.
3. Josephine W. Johnson, from *Year's End* (New York: Simon and Schuster, 1937). Reprinted by permission of the author's estate.
4. Urban T. Holmes, *Ministry and Imagination* (New York:The Seabury Press, 1981) pp.187-8. Used by permission of the author's estate.

Chapter 26
All You Have To Do Is Be
ZEALOUS

I recall an old fable about a lazy frog who ultimately came to a bad end because he would not address himself with any ardor to securing the necessities of life. He expended no effort to engage in the strenuous activity of hunting or pursuing food. Lying indolently on a lily pad, with his mouth open in anticipation, whenever anyone asked him what he was doing he would simply say, "I'm waiting for Providence to send me a fly." No fly ever came, and eventually the frog vanished from the scene, leaving nothing behind but a bad example. As with all fables, there is a moral to be noted—in this case having to do with what is necessary for anyone to reach any desirable goal in life. Apathy just won't do it. It takes effort—and not just minimal effort. Wholeheartedness, ardor, passion, fervor—in short, *zeal*—is called for in order to propel oneself along the trajectory of a vital life experience. Being perfunctory and lackadaisical is not an acceptable way to live. It is not acceptable to you and me as we consider our options; and it is certainly not acceptable to the God who made us and the Lord who directs us, as some emphatic words of Scripture indicate:

> I know your deeds, that you are neither cold nor hot. I wish that you were either one or the other! So because you are lukewarm—neither cold nor hot—I am about to spit you out of my mouth" (Revelation 3:15).

Think about the expression employed in that verse! It's one thing to look forward to a day of judgment and to hope that the words we will hear declared to us then will be the blessed expression, "Well done; enter into the joy of thy Lord"(Matthew 25:21 KJV). But it's another thing altogether to picture God as passing judgment on us by exclaiming something like "*Puh-tooey!*"as He spits out the tepid, tasteless, flat and flavorless stuff that is supposed to represent a vital, tangy life. God never intended for anyone to be bland and half-hearted. Our Creator designed us to *be* something, and to be that something with vigorous earnestness! The final direction for the recipe for life, then, would appropriately be something like "Flavor with *zeal,* and stir well!"

To be Zealous Is To Aspire AFTER God

Two mindsets may be commonly observed among people today, either of which can have the same sad effect of blunting our *zeal.*

One is simple *stolidness.* There really isn't much possibility of being thrillingly committed to and involved in the pursuit of life if one has no sense of a captivating and motivating urge that irresistibly compels one on to fulfillment. There's a common saying that advises quite forthrightly, "Don't sweat the small stuff." And if one is persuaded in one's heart that, in essence, pretty well everything is small stuff, and that virtually nothing is worth breaking into a sweat over, then where's the incentive to address anything with any sort of intensity or fervency?

And the other deficient approach to life I would define as *trepidation*—a condition in which a person is simply cowed or overawed by everything around him or her; where the response to life's happenings and events is something like, "Well, it's all bigger and stronger than I am, so all I can do is to let it roll over me and just do the best I can. You can't fight it; and if you can't beat 'em, join 'em. What will be will be." It has been observed that the two extremes that people are in danger of falling prey to when faced with the demands and opportunities of life, are: hot heads that may lead them to act foolishly; and cold feet that could prevent them from acting at all. To that I would add that what we need, then, are warm hearts and stirred spirits that will inspire us to act *zealously.* When we are eagerly pursuing a realized fellowship with the God who is at the center of our lives, when we are truly aspiring after Him, we will have the incentive and the confidence to live all of life with verve and vitality.

I share a personal experience that I think reflects upon the two attitudes I have noted.

A number of years ago, during some free time while visiting on business in a town some distance from my home, I had the good fortune to discover a used book store. I was delighted to have the opportunity to do some browsing therein, and spent an enjoyable time doing just that. I don't remember much about that experience now. I don't recall the name of the store, or what the proprietor looked like, or whether credit cards were accepted or cash was required. Significantly, though, what I do remember very clearly, are the *titles* of two particular books that I discovered sitting next to each other on one of the shelves in that shop.

The title of the one book was simply, *The Riddle of Life.* And as I think of that even now it brings back the sense that I had when I first read it that this reveals a certain temperament that I can only associate with diffidence and uncertainty. It seems to me that if that title represents my take on life, then what I am saying is that life is either too complicated or too daunting, or too ambiguous or too unfathomable for me to figure it out and for me to do much of anything about it except to "go with the flow" and try to survive and cope as best I can. Life is just too complex and contrary, too much of a *riddle,* for me to address it with any degree of assertiveness and confidence. I find that book's title, and its consequent outlook on life, rather insipid and unappealing.

But that is in sharp contrast with the second volume, which stood immediately next to the first one and that differed from it in one very significant way, namely, just a one-word change in the title. This book was called—not hesitatingly or backwardly, the *Riddle of Life*—but boldly and encouragingly, the *Challenge of Life. That,* I thought, is the only way to go! With God at the center of my life, with my focus on fulfilling my destiny in Him, life should indeed be a grand adventure of discovery and openness and possibility—indeed, of *challenge*—permeated with a spirit of *zeal* in all that I do.

To Be Zealous Is To Be Anchored IN God

I am always impressed by stories of personal faith and belief when I hear them or read them; and there is no source for declarations of zealous believing and acting that impresses me more than the Book of Psalms. Time and time again I see recorded there expressions of a fervency of belief by which I am encouraged in my own ongoing journey of life. I can illustrate this with a reference to one turn of biblical language in particular.

Among the several words commonly used in and throughout the Psalms to convey the idea of supplicating God—of calling on Him or crying out to Him in prayer—one particular Hebrew word, *shava,* is employed in several instances. Now, I suppose it is a truism to observe that one does not actually pray, one does not genuinely call upon God to reveal His presence and power, unless one has at least some degree of faith that God will hear and respond. Indeed, "without faith it is impossible to please God, because anyone who comes to Him must believe that He exists and that He rewards those who earnestly seek Him" (Hebrews 11:6). The need for *earnestness,* thus, would indicate that one's prayer life could be said to be measurable in terms of the depth and quality of the *zeal* with which one engages in it. And whenever *shava* is used in the Psalms, I am impressed that that is the case; because that word does not mean simply to call upon God in the way in which one might commonly place a telephone call, or to address God in the perfunctory way that serves merely as an opening conversational gambit. Rather, it has a much more intense meaning—a meaning that is more like our English language notion of hollering, or making a commotion, to attract attention. In fact, it might even be translated in common vernacular terms as something like *"Hey!"* or *"Halloo!"* It has a quality of boldness and insistence about it that speaks of a firm determination to be heard and a firm expectation that there will be a response on the part of the one hailed. And it always reminds me of a little play on words that a certain minister friend of mine used to enjoy pointing out in connection with a certain hymn. I refer to the hymn, "How Firm a Foundation," at the place in the opening stanza where the hymn-writer asks the rhetorical question, "What more can He say than to you He hath said—to you who to Jesus for refuge have fled?" My friend was fond of pointing to and factoring out the expression "you who to Jesus," and employing that as a rather unusual form of communication, *i.e.*, "yoo-hoo to Jesus!" But for all its deliberate facetiousness, that little play on words really contains a valid biblical truth, because if one is praying with real *zeal*, and one's approach to God is marked by a firm and convinced belief in God's care for us and His readiness to hear us and respond to us, then one may indeed have the confidence to unreservedly speak out to gain the attention and the concern of a strong and compassionate Lord and to do so in the honest spirit of calling "Yoo-hoo to Jesus!" And I am convinced in this matter that the level of intensity employed in our calling upon God is a direct reflection of the depth of our belief in Him and in His readiness to touch and empower our lives by His grace.

To Be Zealous Is To Continue TOWARDS God

Some years ago, the Xerox Corporation published a study on the sales performance of their field representatives. The results showed, interestingly, that while such characteristics as personality type, social skills and physical appearance were important in determining success rates, the one most significant factor that set the winners apart from the more plodding also-rans was an easily identified practice. It was simply that the premium performers made an average of five more calls per day than their less successful counterparts. Reading that statistic makes me wonder: why was that? What was it that led those winning agents to go on beyond the efforts of their fellows and make those five extra, crucial contacts? What motivated and impelled them to rise above the pack? I would quite frankly call it a facet of *zeal.* I would recognize it as the determination to simply continue in one's endeavors, and not be satisfied with mediocrity, even when one is tired or on the point of discouragement, or—perhaps just as importantly and possibly more dangerously—even when one is gratifyingly flushed with some degree of apparent success. It may be easy to rationalize one's way into a state of contentment with a level of accomplishment, and even a level of *being,* that is actually closer to mediocrity than to excellence. If it was important, as the Xerox survey shows it certainly was, for company employees to continue to bear down to reach out for excellence in career attainment; then how much more important is it for us in our pursuit of personal fullness and wholeness to show a similar spirit of steadfastness and staying power. In fact, we might take as a personal instruction the parting advice that the apostles Paul and Barnabas gave to an eager group of disciples who, after having heard the instruction of the Gospel concerning the will of God for their salvation and wholeness, besought the preachers for one last, further word. Significantly and succinctly, the biblical record gives us the apostles' response: "Paul and Barnabas . . . talked with them, and urged them to *continue in the grace of God"* Acts 13:43). That is the same sentiment that Paul expresses elsewhere when he urges widows, who have no means of support and are totally dependent upon God, to *"continue in prayers and supplications"* (1 Timothy 5:5), that God would hear and answer their petitions. That sounds to me like the biblical equivalent of a pep talk, advising the equivalent of *"Pour it on!"* It's a call to live not tepidly or half-heartedly, but *zealously.*

To Be Zealous Is To Delight IN God

"Delight yourself in the Lord," the Psalmist writes (Psalm 37:4); which admonition you might expand to say "Really let the deep joyfulness of responding to your Creator/Redeemer God and His plan for your life permeate your whole being to the place where it sort of percolates through your entire person making you fulfillingly and *zestfully* truly alive." The more you delight in the Lord and pursue the calling with which He challenges you, the more you will increase in those qualities and characteristics after which you aspire. And the more that that is the case, the brighter will glow the *zeal* we possess and express.

Arnold Beisser makes an observation that ties in very well with the notion of zealous delight as a part of any experience that is truly vital and growth-promoting. He uses the analogy of a roller coaster—an instrument of entertainment that, for many, might more appropriately be described as an instrument of *terror!* I can still recall very vividly an encounter with a roller coaster that I had that led to a sincere vow on my part that has never been broken. I am sure I am not alone as a parent in having had the experience of yielding to the pleas of an eager child to accompany him or her on one of those death-defying (or death-*tempting!)* rides. In my case it was my daughter, aged about nine, who persuaded me that it would be a wonderful adventure for us to share a ride on some sort of a rocket at the fair. Bravely and foolishly I agreed, and soon we were off. I was vaguely aware of her screams as she sat beside me—whether screams of pleasure or panic I could not tell—but as we alternately soared and plummeted, and twisted and careened through the air my attention was really most singularly focused on my own sensations. I sat there gray-faced and petrified, silently making a profoundly solemn vow: *"Never again!"*—a vow that I have kept inviolate over all the years since and which I intend to keep intact for the rest of my life. And it is against the background of the kind of experience that my daughter and I shared that day that I can appreciate what Beisser writes:

> On a roller coaster, it is fun only if you go with each experience and allow yourself to discover all there is in it. If you are set against the experience, the most you can hope for is survival, and you will miss the richness of the ups and downs.[1]

Out of my great antipathy towards roller coasters, I can appreciate very much what that observation means. I certainly missed "the richness of the ups and downs" on my ride, and for sure the only thing on my mind was survival! I cannot conceive of anyone joyfully and willingly entering into a roller coaster experience and calling it fun. But I know that people do it. I am fascinated to visit the fair each fall and to walk through the midway where I see people having the time of their lives on the most incredible rides imaginable. I cannot share their point of view; but their actions help me to grasp and appreciate the principle that Beisser enunciates concerning it all; and I am led to attain a deeper insight into the heartfelt experience of delight in giving oneself unreservedly and *zealously* to the life that God wills for us. "Taste and see that the Lord is good," the Psalmist urges (Psalm 34:8). That's the only way you're ever going to prove the reality of living intensely and to the full—by plunging into the grace of God and finding the *delight* that zealous participation in His life provides.

And, by the way, something more about delight. It is truly a wonderful thing to be so wrapped up in the pursuit of God's design and so enthralled with the God who has called us to our pursuit that we delight to know and follow Him. But consider that our relationship with God is a two-way street, and that there is, then, a second party who can also enter into a sense of pleasure and elation over the progress we make towards *becoming*. And that party is God Himself!

What might it be like for God, as a caring and concerned Parent, to watch the developing lives of His children, and rejoice in their successes? What might it be like for God's heart to be gladdened by the choices we make, the values we espouse, the words we speak, the deeds we perform? Does it sound too anthropomorphic to say that, like a loving father at a little league game who is surprised by joy when his young slugger son or daughter steps up to the plate and delivers a crucial, game-winning hit, God watches to see how we will perform in the game of life, and cheers wildly when we come through nobly and well? Does it fail to do justice to the immutability and almightiness of God to picture Him as watching and waiting in solicitous love to see how we turn out, rather than simply standing by as the great Unmoved Mover whose mysterious omniscience precludes any possibility of breathless wonder and pleasure regarding human affairs? I am not in any way questioning the utter omnipotence of the great Creator God who has made us and sent us forth into life. His wisdom, knowledge and power are infinite, and He, as the One who was and is and is to be, is eternal in all the attributes of His deity. But I am also not hesitant to ascribe to this great God at least the compassion, and the yearning love, and the proud joy of a parent in His role as our Heavenly Father. And I feel encouraged by the thought that something I might do in my own experience might gladden the heart of God and give Him profound pleasure. I know that people sometimes speak of "disappointing" God through the unworthy or ignoble things they choose to love, and do, and, ultimately, to be. If that can be the case, then why is it not just as legitimate to speak of "pleasing" God through the right and lovely things that we seek after and embrace? Isn't that what St. Paul was talking about doing when he spoke about offering up to God fragrant sacrifices on the altars of our heart, in imitation of Jesus, who "did constantly those things which pleased His Father" (Ephesians 5:2)? And if we can please God by our response to the challenges and difficulties and opportunities of life, then can we not simply say that we can look forward to His taking delight in us and our living? I think so! And what a tremendously profound and thrilling and uplifting thought it is to believe that my fumbling faithfulness to the calling of God, my heartfelt, and earnest, and *zealous* desire to press on to know and serve and obey Him ever more worthily, causes joy in the heart of my Creator/Redeemer God! What an incentive, indeed, to a life of *zeal* in the service of the Most High!

"It is good to be zealously affected in a good thing," St. Paul wrote (Galatians 4:18, KJV). The "good thing" in which we are affected and involved is nothing less than the life whose dimensions we have been examining in all our considerations to this point—the fullness of *being* for which our Creator designed us. Let us pursue that goal, in all its rich totality, *zealously*.

Notes

[1] Arnold Beisser, *Flying Without Wings* (New York: Bantam Books, 1990) p.111.